by Alan MacDonald

Illustrated by Clive Goddard

Scholastic Children's Books,
Euston House, 24 Eversholt Street,
London, NW1 1DB, UK
A division of Scholastic Ltd
London ~ New York ~ Toronto ~ Sydney ~ Auckland
Mexico City ~ New Delhi ~ Hong Kong

Published in the UK by Scholastic Ltd, 2001

10 digit ISBN 0 439 99911 1
13 digit ISBN 978 0439 99911 3

Typeset by M Rules
Printed in the UK by CPI Bookmarque Ltd, Croydon, CR0 4TD

17 19 20 18

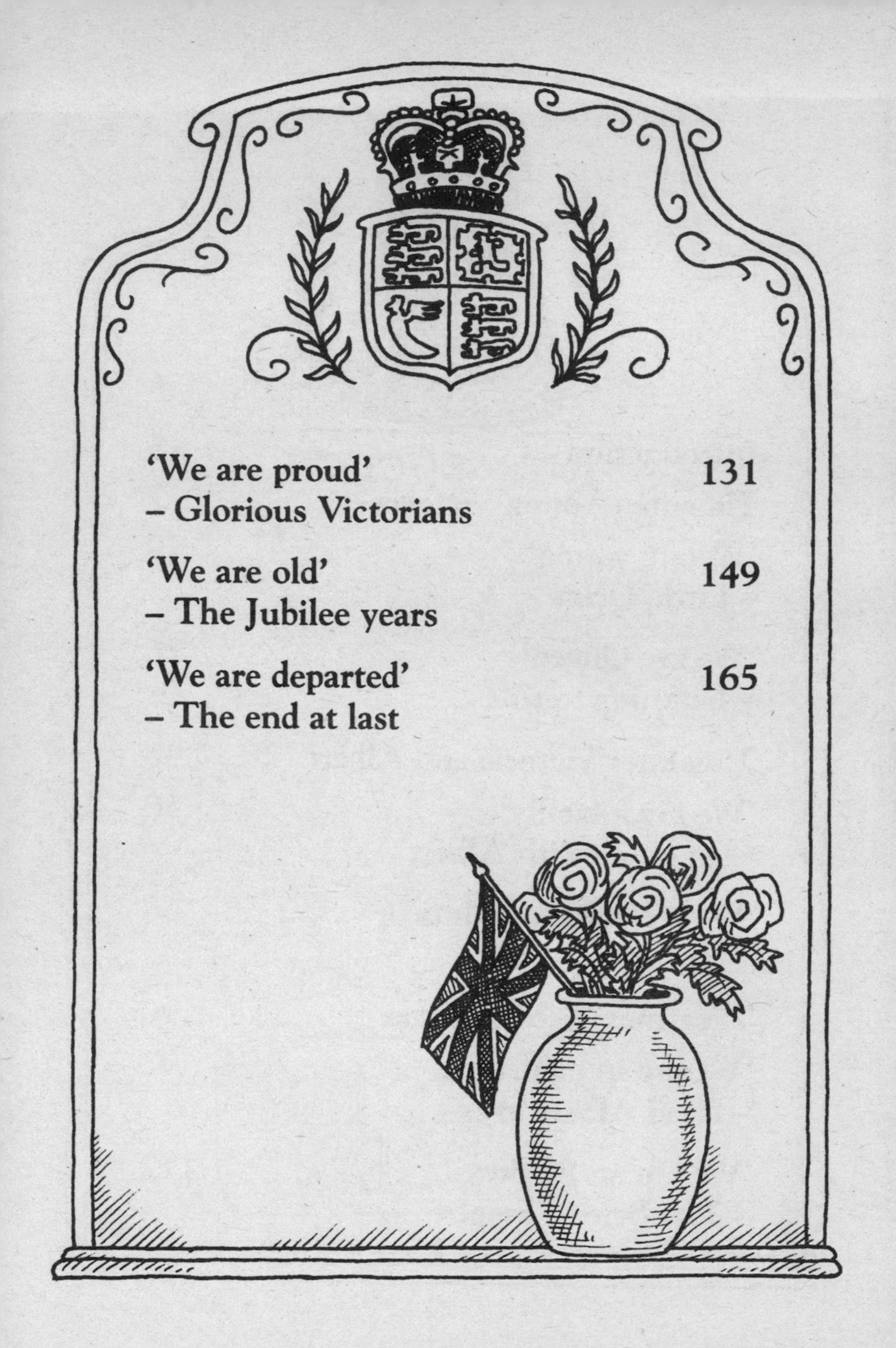

INTRODUCTION

Queen Victoria. This is probably how most people picture her:

A fat little old lady with a face that would turn milk sour. Victoria, as we all know, was dead famous for being strict, stuffy and disapproving. A queen who wore only black for 30 years and was as gloomy as a graveyard. Her most famous saying is:

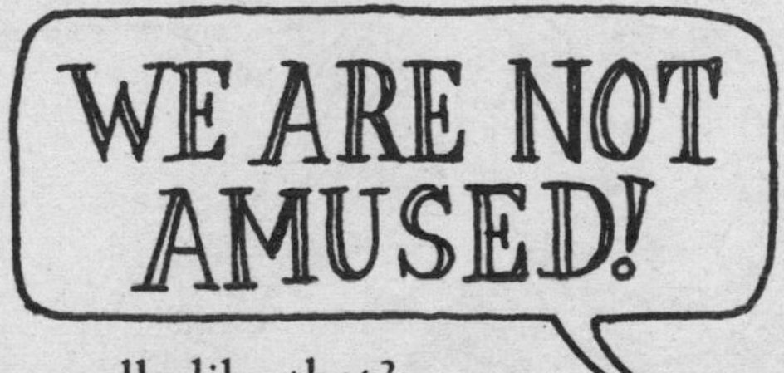

But was she really like that?

Well, did you know that Queen Victoria often smiled? One reason we usually picture her looking grumpy is because Victorian cameras took so long to take a picture. By the time the Queen was snapped her smile had usually faded to a bored frown!

In fact when she first became Queen, young Vicky was a lively 18-year-old, who liked games, going to the theatre and dancing. The fact is she was often amused, as you'll find out in this book. For instance, did you know that:

- She had Albert's potty cleaned every day – even though he was dead.
- She often went out in disguise.
- She once let an African chief wear her lace cap.

Victoria ruled England for a record-breaking 63 years. In that time the world changed out of all recognition. Victoria was born in the age of the stagecoach and went out in the age of the aeroplane. As you read *The Hard Times* newspaper and dip into the Queen's diary (the *secret* version) you'll meet the real Victoria, the one behind all those black looks. Read on for some gripping stories of bloomers, big hats and the mighty British Empire.

TIMELINE: YOUNG VICTORIA
1819: VICTORIA BORN AT KENSINGTON PALACE.
IT'S A GIRL!
1820: A DEADLY YEAR FOR ROYALS. VICTORIA'S FATHER, EDWARD DUKE OF KENT, DIES. 'MAD' KING GEORGE III POPS OFF.
ERK!
EEK!
1829: LONDON'S FIRST POLICE FORCE STARTED. NICKNAMED 'PEELERS' OR 'BOBBIES'.
MORNIN' BOB
MORNIN' BOB
MORNIN' BOB
MORNIN' BOB
1830: 'UNCLE KING' - GEORGE IV - TURNS UP HIS TOES. WILLIAM IV - 'SAILOR BILL' - TAKES OVER THE HELM.
ARG!
HA-HAR!
1833: SLAVERY ABOLISHED THROUGHOUT THE BRITISH EMPIRE.
AND ABOUT TIME TOO!
1834: GRUEL DAYS - POOR LAW CREATES ROTTEN WORKHOUSES. HOUSES OF PARLIAMENT BURN DOWN.
SERVES 'EM RIGHT!

1835: VICTORIA TOURS ENGLAND AND SEES POOR PEOPLE.
OOH LOOK, THERE'S ONE!
1837: SAILOR BILL SINKS. 18-YEAR-OLD VICTORIA BECOMES QUEEN.
GLUG!
WHO, ME?
1839: THE BEDCHAMBER CRISIS - VICTORIA PUTS HER FOOT DOWN. SNAP! FIRST CAMERA DEVELOPED.
SAY CHEESE!
SHAN'T!
STAMP!
1840: VICTORIA MARRIES HANDSOME ALBERT. FIRST POSTAGE STAMPS - PENNY BLACKS - BEARING VICTORIA'S HEAD. VICTORIA'S FIRST CHILD, PRINCESS VICKY BORN.
1841: BERTIE, PRINCE OF WALES BORN. HE'LL HAVE A LONG WAIT TO BECOME KING.
POO...

In 1819 a coach rattled its way along through Germany on its way to France. The driver was in a hurry. Inside, his heavily pregnant wife bounced around on the bumpy road and wished the journey would end.

The driver was the Duke of Kent and his wife, the Duchess, was carrying a child. A gypsy had foretold that one day the baby would become Queen of England. At the time the prediction didn't seem very likely, but the Duke wasn't taking any chances. He wanted his baby to be born in England, not somewhere on the road to Calais.

The parents made it home and the baby was born on 24 May at Kensington Palace. Her grandmother called her 'the May flower' but Victoria wouldn't have won any beautiful baby contests. Even her Dad admitted that.

Baby Vicky was a bit of a podge, but then she followed her royal family in that respect. At the time, Vicky was only fifth in line to the throne. King George III had plenty of ugly relatives who had their greedy eyes on the crown.

Heir today, queen tomorrow

With all those fat uncles around, it's surprising that Victoria ever got to be queen. Yet, as it turned out, fate handed her the crown on a silver plate. None of her uncles produced a child who could be heir to the throne. It's true Uncle Clarence did have lots of children but they either died or didn't count because they weren't his wife's children. Next in the pecking order came Vicky's dad, and when he died that left Victoria as the heir apparent (the bottom most likely to sit on the throne). Of course, in 1819 when little Vicky was born, no one guessed that things would turn out this way. Vicky was a royal baby but not especially important.

For now there was the small matter of naming the baby. It wasn't a happy start.

'I name this child'

Did you know that the Victorian age was almost called something else? It could have been the Alexandrinan age (a bit of a mouthful) or the Elizabethan age (rather confusing as there'd been one of those already.) It was all because of the row over the baby's name.

Imagine the scene – the happy occasion of a royal christening. The proud parents – the Duke and Duchess of Kent – are there with the baby. A handful of royal relatives have come to witness the occasion. Among them the godfather, fat Uncle George, is looking grumpy – even though he'll soon be king.

The christening takes place at Kensington Palace where red velvet curtains have been hastily added to make the room look more regal. Jealous Uncle George has said a state christening with all the trimmings is totally out of the question. He doesn't want his niece stealing all the attention. The Archbishop takes the plump child in his arms and pauses over the font. 'I name this child. . .' he says and turns to Fat George.

'Alexandrina,' comes the short reply.

There's an embarrassed silence. The parents had chosen a long list of royal names for their bouncing babe – Victoria Georgina Alexandrina Charlotte Augusta – but George isn't following the script. Nervously the father suggests Charlotte and Augusta. George turns him down flat. 'Elizabeth?' A shake of the head.

Fat George doesn't want his godchild bearing any of the traditional royal names. The baby's mother, the Duchess of Kent, bursts into tears. Glaring at her, Fat George mumbles, 'Give her the mother's name also then.'

So, in the middle of a seething family row, the baby is finally baptized Alexandrina Victoria. As a girl she'll be known as Little Drina – but Victoria will be the name she takes later. On the whim of a plump grumpy uncle the Victorian Age gets its name.

Nineteenth-century Britain

What kind of world did Little Drina grow up in? For a start the monarchy was in a bad way. Fat George IV became king in 1820, but his subjects were more likely to jeer than cheer when he was seen out in his carriage.

More importantly, Victoria was born at a crossroads in history, when rural England was being replaced by a new world of machines and factories. The Industrial Revolution was sweeping Britain and re-shaping the landscape – not always for the better.

Change was in the air and new inventions were making their mark.

1 The first WC or water closet is on the market (though most families still use a bucket).

2 Parts of London are now lit by gas lights.

3 New roads mean that mail coaches can travel at a breath-taking 16 – 19 km an hour.

4 Baby Victoria is one of the first lucky ones to be vaccinated against smallpox.

Meanwhile, in the slums of London and the north, poor children go on dying of smallpox and other dire diseases like cholera and dysentery. But who cares about them? Certainly Little Drina doesn't meet any poor people. Her childhood is filled with dolls, pets and taking tea with Mamma.

A sad life?

In later life, Victoria was fond of saying she'd had 'a sad dull childhood', but it's hard to see what she had to grumble about. Compared to children from poor families her life was a happy, idle existence. Here's a typical day when she was four years old.

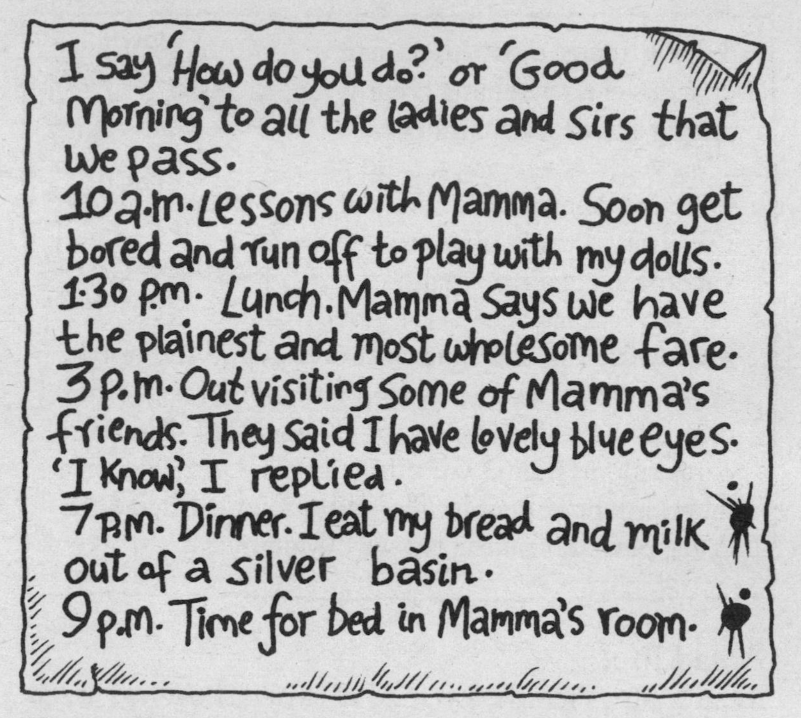

You might imagine that Victoria would have been a serious, solemn child, but you'd have been wrong. All the stories suggest that she was a proper little madam. When she played on the lawn in front of her house at Kensington Palace, a crowd often gathered to watch her through the railings. Little Drina used to play to the gallery, curtsying and kissing her hand to her public. Sometimes she would run over to talk to her future subjects and have to be dragged away by her disapproving nurse, Boppy (as Vicky called her).

Uncle King

When she was seven years old Victoria had her first visit to her Uncle King – George IV. Remembering how badly he'd behaved at the christening her mother must have been nervous. She needn't have worried – Victoria charmed her fat foolish uncle. Kissing his face can't have been easy for a seven-year-old girl. The King was a ridiculous old man who wore a wig and plastered his face with make-up. In a letter, Victoria wrote:

> *The King took me by the hand, saying, 'Give me your little paw.' He was large and gouty but with a wonderful dignity and charm of manner.*

Naturally Victoria couldn't be too rude about her Uncle King. The Duke of Wellington who was also present had no such qualms. He remembered the meeting differently.

The King was very drunk, very blackguard, very foolish, very much out of temper at times – and a very great bore!

Spoilt rotten

We haven't mentioned Victoria's dear papa since the christening. That's because the Duke of York died the year after Little Drina was born. With only a nurse and her doting Mamma to look after her, Victoria was spoilt rotten. Everyone worshipped 'the poor little fatherless child' and Victoria took full advantage. Screaming fits and tantrums regularly exploded in the nursery. Once, one of her playmates – Lady Jane Elliot – had the nerve to play with Vicky's toys. Victoria fixed her with an icy glare and said:

You must not touch those, they are mine, and I may call you Jane, but you must not call me Victoria.

More often it was dear mamma or her tutors who suffered from the tiny tyrant.

Eventually Nurse Boppy – who was fighting a losing battle – was replaced by a governess called Louise Lehzen. Lehzen was made of sterner stuff and set about trying to impose some discipline on the spoilt Princess. She soon took a firm line on the screaming and foot-stamping. Victoria even had to apologize to her maid when she was naughty or rude. There was still bargaining at bedtime and often it took a lot of persuasion to get Vicky up in the morning. When forced to put on her stockings by Lehzen, she would complain in tragic tones:

As a little girl, Victoria was a chubby bundle of mischief. Of course her childhood was hardly a normal one. How many other children have a collection of 132 wooden puppets to play with? She didn't go to school or have friends round to play. In fact she hardly saw any friends of her own age at all. But there were advantages to being a princess. Here are a few of the highlights you might have seen if you were able to take a peek in young Vicky's photo album.

School for Royals

As we mentioned, Victoria didn't have to go to school like other kids – school came to her. Whereas most schools have lots of children and a handful of teachers, Victoria's schooling involved lots of teachers and only one pupil – the Princess herself. This had its disadvantages. When a teacher asked a question, Victoria couldn't hope that someone else would put their hand up first.

The tutor in charge of the Princess's schooling was the Reverend George Davys. As a vicar, George taught Vicky religion (or at least the Church of England version), while a long line of other tutors were called in to handle other subjects. Victoria's school timetable included Maths, German, French, Italian, Latin, Music, Dancing, Drawing and Calligraphy (lettering).

Victoria was a whizz at modern languages, pretty handy with a paintbrush but bottom of the class at Latin. It may sound a narrow sort of education, but girls weren't supposed to be too bright anyway. As long as a young lady could dance, say 'Pass the cake' in French and embroider a hanky, she was considered quite educated enough to get married. The idea of women becoming doctors or engineers in Victoria's day was considered as mad as men landing on the moon. In any case, Victoria's schooling was much better than most children could expect. Take a look at what you had to suffer if you went to an ordinary school.

School daze

Not all children went to school in Victoria's day, and those that did probably wished they'd stayed at home. There were no government-run schools like today. Schools were either public schools (where you had to pay) or charity or church schools based on the Sunday School movement.

Some poor children went to 'ragged schools' where they learned the three R's – Reading, Riting and Rithmetic (but obviously not spelling). Ragged schools provided free basic schooling, clothing and food for thousands of poor children.

The school day began at nine and lasted eight long hours until five o' clock, starting and ending with mumbled prayers. Much of the teaching was done by the children chanting aloud their times tables or other facts.

Discipline made joining the army look like a picnic. No talking was allowed in class and if you got your sums wrong you'd end up standing in the corner wearing the dunce's cap. Teachers were allowed to hit children and some of them thought it was their duty.

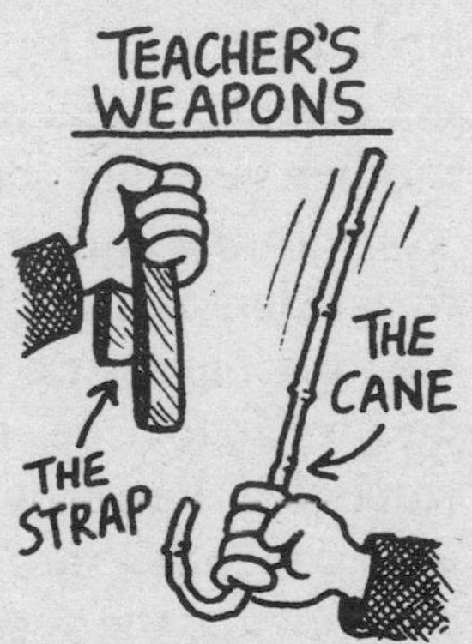

Boys from rich families who attended posh boarding schools weren't any better off. A lot of bullying went on unchecked by the teachers and there were stories of children being roasted over fires or burnt with cigar butts. (A jolly book called *Tom Brown's Schooldays* goes into detail.) If the school bully didn't get you, then the bullying teachers might. The headmaster of Eton school once flogged 72 boys in a row without a tea break!

Girls didn't go to public schools. They were usually taught at home by a governess and learned even less than Victoria. During Victoria's reign the need for properly run schools for all children was gradually recognized. But it wasn't until 1880 that it became law for all five – ten-year-olds to go to school. Just think, if it wasn't for good old Victoria *you* might be sitting at home watching TV!

A bit of an accident

By the time Victoria was ten years old it was clear that none of her fat royal uncles would produce an heir to the throne. The next queen of England would be the plump little Princess. The only problem was that no one had got round to breaking the news to Victoria herself. Her mother said that she rather hoped her daughter would 'come to the knowledge by accident.' Exactly what kind of accident did she have in mind? Maybe she imagined Victoria might trip over a crown in the street one day and try it for size. In the end an 'accident' had to be carefully arranged. Governess Lehzen suggested slipping an extra page into Vicky's history book. By a lucky coincidence the page would show the truth:

From an early age Victoria kept her own diary. In its pages she recorded the momentous occasion when she realized she'd one day be queen.

REAL DIARY EXTRACT

> *I am nearer to the throne than I thought. I will be good.*

It's become Victoria's signature tune – the ten-year-old child who promised to do her duty and be a good queen. But maybe Vicky's secret thoughts weren't quite so goody goody. Not many people know that Queen Victoria's *actual* diary was burned. On her death she left it to her youngest daughter, Beatrice, with instructions to make a copy and burn the original version. We can safely say that Princess Beatrice copied out a watered-down version. She probably left out all the juicy bits and re-wrote anything too rude or revealing. So we can only guess at what Victoria *actually* wrote in her diary. Or use our imaginations. . .

VICTORIA'S SECRET DIARY

11th March 1830
Ha! So it's true – I'm going to be queen one day. Tra-la-la! I knew there was something they were hiding from me. Things are going to change round here

The teenage years

As it turned out, Victoria had only another eight years to wait. Her teenage years were unhappy, mainly because her mother had fallen under the influence of a sneaky creep called Sir John Conroy.

Using his slimy charms, Conroy had already taken control of the Duchess's household, but he had his sights set on a bigger jewel. Knowing that Victoria was still young, Conroy was plotting to become the real power behind the throne. He made sure Victoria and her mamma were kept away from anyone who suspected his nasty plot (the King, for instance).

When Victoria fell seriously ill at Ramsgate, aged 16, creepy Conroy tried to make her sign a document to name him as her private secretary when she became

Queen. But even in illness, young Vicky was stubborn as a mule and refused to sign. Up to the last hour, as King William IV lay dying, Conroy and the Duchess tried to persuade Victoria to accept what Conroy called his 'system' (i.e. 'I give the orders'). Victoria shut herself in her room and refused to listen. Then the next morning the great news came. Unfortunately, since it was 5 a.m. everyone was asleep when the messengers arrived. It took about an hour before 18-year-old Victoria emerged from her bedroom in her dressing gown and slippers. As usual she wrote it all down in her diary.

> *I was awoke at 6 o'clock by Mamma who told me that the Archbishop of Canterbury and Lord Conyngham were here and wished to see me. I got out of bed and went into the sitting room (only in my dressing gown) and alone, and saw them. Lord Conyngham (the Lord Chamberlain) then acquainted me that my poor Uncle, the King, was no more, and had expired at 12 minutes past 2 this morning and consequently that I am Queen.*
>
> REAL DIARY EXTRACT

Maybe the reaction in her uncensored diary was simpler.

Victoria's first act as Queen was to have her bed removed from her dear mamma's room. At last she was free. Well, sort of. . .

'WE ARE QUEEN' – LEARNING TO RULE

Because most pictures of Victoria show her in plump, dumpy old age, it's easy to forget what Victoria was like when she first became queen. Here's a picture to remind you.

The most striking thing about Victoria was not her beauty but her youth. She was still a teenager when she became queen – and the British weren't used to royalty in skirts. No woman had ruled England since Queen Anne over 100 years before.

In her favour, Victoria arrived at a time when the monarchy's popularity was at rock bottom. She could hardly do a worse job than the last three royals to fill the throne.

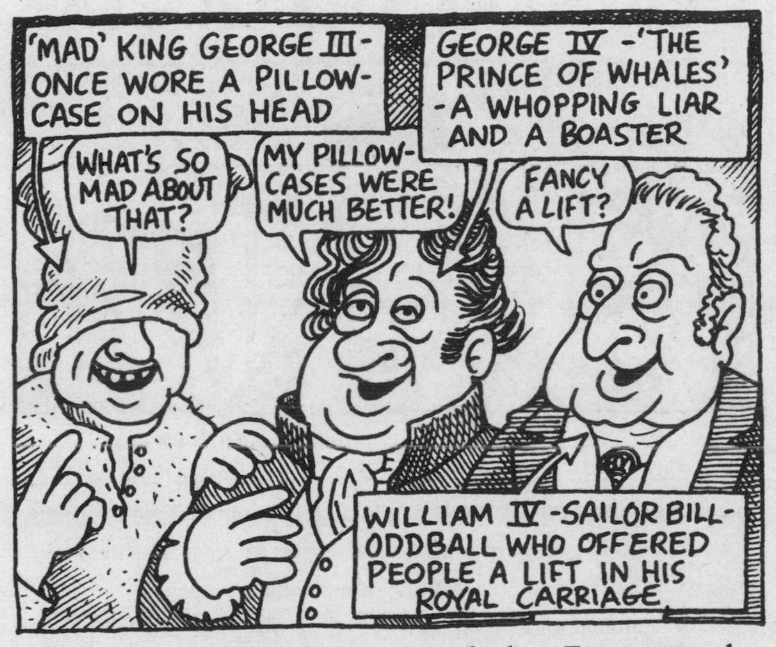

Victoria had several things going for her. For starters she wasn't barking mad like some of her relatives. Also she was young, honest and hard-working. True, having a large doll collection wasn't much of a training for ruling a country, but she was willing to learn. Luckily she found a kindly father figure in her first Prime Minister, Lord Melbourne. In fact all her life Vicky would lean on a series of father figures – Melbourne, Prince Albert, Disraeli and, later, a Scotsman named John Brown, who often had to lean on other people when he was drunk.

More of them later. First Victoria had to be crowned.

THE HARD TIMES

28th June 1838

GOD SAVE THE QUEEN!

In an affecting ceremony at Westminster Abbey this morning, the young Queen was crowned in front of 10,000 guests. Looking majestic in her crimson robes and a small diamond circlet on her head, the young Queen was a picture of dignity.

From a quarter to seven, lords and ladies had thronged the Abbey, their necks and hands glittering with diamonds.

The weather was fine and all along the route the Queen's coach was greeted by the thunderous cheers of her subjects.

'I really cannot say how proud I feel to be the Queen of such a nation,' said Victoria, before rushing back home to give her pet dog, Dash, a much needed bath.

A royal blunder

Actually, the coronation was not the triumph the newspapers reported. In fact, it was dogged by a catalogue of blunders.

The problem was that hardly anyone – least of all Victoria herself – knew what was supposed to happen. With no proper rehearsal for the main players, things were bound to go wrong – and sure enough they did...

1 Victoria's coronation ring was forced on to the wrong finger by the Archbishop. Afterwards Victoria had to bathe her finger in iced water to get the ring off.

2 Doddery 88-year-old Lord Rolle lived up to his name by tripping and tumbling down the steps when he tried to touch the Queen's crown. A wit remarked that Lord Rolle only held his title on the condition of taking a tumble at every coronation.

3 The Bishop of Bath and Wells accidently turned over two pages of the ceremony together and told Victoria it was all over. After a long delay she had to be brought back to go over it again.

4 In the meantime Victoria was taken to St Edward's Chapel, which looked more like a picnic site. Bottles of wine and sandwiches had been left on the altar by lords having a late breakfast.

5 The Bishop of Durham gave Victoria the orb too early in the ceremony. 'What am I to do with it?' asked a puzzled Victoria.

So Queen Victoria's 64-year reign started with a series of blunders. Unfortunately things didn't get much better for young Vicky. She was soon caught up in the nasty whiff of scandal.

The case of Lady Flora's bulge

The first test of the new young queen involved a spot of scandal and a Lady in Waiting. Lady Flora Hastings was a member of Victoria's mum's household and the Queen couldn't stand her. Victoria had grown more and more distant from her dear mamma and was keen to finally get rid of Sir John Conroy who she referred to as the Demon.

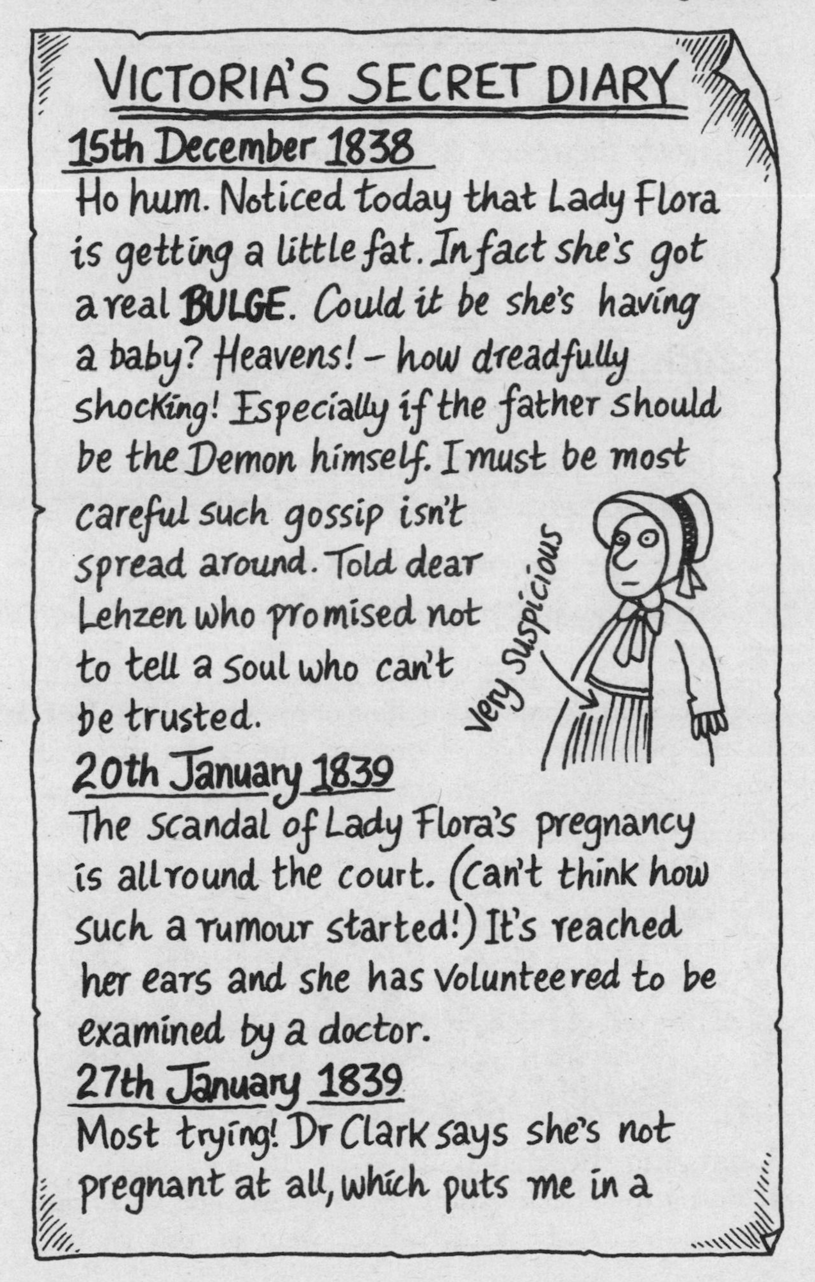

VICTORIA'S SECRET DIARY

15th December 1838

Ho hum. Noticed today that Lady Flora is getting a little fat. In fact she's got a real **BULGE**. Could it be she's having a baby? Heavens! – how dreadfully shocking! Especially if the father should be the Demon himself. I must be most careful such gossip isn't spread around. Told dear Lehzen who promised not to tell a soul who can't be trusted.

20th January 1839

The scandal of Lady Flora's pregnancy is all round the court. (Can't think how such a rumour started!) It's reached her ears and she has volunteered to be examined by a doctor.

27th January 1839

Most trying! Dr Clark says she's not pregnant at all, which puts me in a

rather awkward spot (though of course I never breathed a word of gossip).
Asked to see Lady Flora but now the wretched woman says she's too ill to come.

20th July 1839

How everything goes against me! Lady Flora has died and I'm sure just to spite me. Her swollen stomach turned out to be cancer of the liver. Well, anyone can make a mistake!

Victoria didn't come up smelling of roses from this affair. In the public eye Lady Flora was cast as the wronged woman and Victoria as the heartless queen. A week before Flora died, the Queen went to Ascot races and got a nasty reception.

Changing the Bed Ladies

It wasn't long before another storm blew up. This time the Ladies of the Bedchamber were at the centre.

(Victoria had lots of Ladies who helped her dress and do things that queens can't possibly do by themselves.)

The Bedchamber Question sounds completely potty to us today, but it managed to bring down a government. The problem arose when Victoria's favourite, Lord Melbourne, was to be replaced as Prime Minister. The newcomer, Sir Robert Peel, was a Tory. Victoria herself was a Whig and all the Ladies of the Queen's Bedchamber were the same. (The Whigs were a political party later known as the Liberals.) Even worse, Victoria felt he lacked good manners. When feeling awkward his feet used to perform a stiff little dance on the carpet. Understandably, Peel wasn't too happy that all the Queen's Ladies were cheering for the opposition party. Victoria, meanwhile, couldn't see that it was any of his business. The argument between Peel and the Queen soon reached deadlock.

Victoria may have been young but Peel soon found she was stubborn. Even the Tory Duke of Wellington, who'd beaten Napoleon at Waterloo, found he'd met his match in Victoria. In the end Peel said he could not form a government under these conditions and Victoria got her beloved Melbourne back as Prime Minister. The Queen was happy. She'd prevented a change of government – and all over a bunch of chambermaids. This kind of thing couldn't happen today as monarchs aren't supposed to have political views. Imagine our present queen telling the world:

'HOW WE LAUGHED' – Queen Victoria was amused

The popular idea of Queen Victoria is that she never smiled or laughed. Certainly she didn't have a sense of humour. Or did she?

In fact Victoria often found things funny and rather than tittering politely she had a deep belly laugh.

Once, when she was sitting for the sculptor Mr Gibson, he asked her if he could measure her mouth. 'Oh certainly,' replied the Queen, 'if I can only keep it still and not laugh.' But the request was so unexpected that the Queen found it impossible to keep a straight face. Every time she closed her mouth she burst out laughing again.

A day in the life

Victoria's daily life during the early years of her reign was blissfully happy. She led a simple life – riding, eating, dancing, and the humdrum business of running a country. And always always there was her dear Lord Melbourne.

VICTORIA'S SECRET DIARY

Morning - sat with Lord M while he read letters from abroad. He is always so amusing. He told me he never carries a watch. 'I always ask the servant what o'clock it is and he tells me what he likes.'

Afternoon - went out riding as usual. Lord M says I look very elegant in my velvet riding habit with a top hat and a little veil. He always rides beside me of course.

Back in time for a game of shuttlecock before dinner.

Dinner - Lord M always sits on my left. What a wretched nuisance I must talk to other people too! After dinner the men join us to talk in the drawing room. Lord M in wonderful form! So amusing!

Bedtime - another tiring day over. Who'd be Queen of England?

Manners

Victoria was very keen on good manners. Victorians had rules for everything from how to address the Queen to the number of knives you needed for dinner. No one was permitted to sit down whilst talking to the Queen unless she asked them – which she rarely did. Even Victoria herself didn't escape the demands of etiquette. One trial she had to endure was speaking to every guest after dinner. One of them, a Mr Greville, later recorded his gripping conversation with the Queen...

But this thrilling life couldn't go on for ever. People were saying that the young Queen should get married. She was so fond of spending time with the Prime Minister that people in the street were starting to call, 'Mrs Melbourne!' after her. Something had to be done. And after all it was the Queen's royal duty to have a child who would be the next king or queen. Victoria, however, wasn't keen to get married. In any case, the list of suitors boiled down to two.

Cousin George was never really in the running. Victoria couldn't see herself marrying one of her own subjects – it would be too humiliating! Anyway she liked her men to be dashing and handsome. That pointed to Albert.

He was also Victoria's cousin and had been groomed to marry her most of his life. Yet not everyone was enthusiastic about the match. Lord Melbourne remarked:

Besides, would the country accept a German prince? More to the point, could Victoria accept anyone?

Victoria had met her cousin before and liked Albert, but things were different now that she was Queen. After her strict childhood, she was enjoying her freedom. She was in no hurry to find a husband who might try to tell her what to do. However, things would change when she set her eyes on Albert. Victoria couldn't resist a slim waist and a pair of manly moustachios. Maybe her private diary recorded her change of heart.

odious the subject is! I don't wish to meet Albert. If I do meet him, I'll have to decide whether to marry him or not. And if I do decide to marry him, I'll have to propose! (He can hardly propose to me, I'm the Queen!) I'd much rather just keep my dear Dash instead. You can tell a dog to 'Sit' and they do what you say. In any case, I'm too old for Albert. (By several months at least.)

10th October 1839

Albert arrived at 7.30 this evening. I met him on the staircase. Cannot put my feelings into words. He is so handsome. I've sketched him from memory.

He has a beautiful figure, broad in the shoulders and a fine slim waist. In short, I find him fascinating. Oh – his brother Ernest was there too.

With Victoria's change of heart, it wasn't long before the marriage was settled. Victoria summoned Albert to a private audience with her. She then proposed in these words:

Albert didn't go down on bended knee. In fact he didn't have much choice in the matter. It never even occurred to Victoria that he might say no. After all he was just a tinpot German prince and she was the Queen of Great Britain.

Albert consented and the match was made. For him it meant leaving his home, his country and his people for a strange foreign land where he wasn't totally welcome. For Victoria it was quite simple – she was in love!

The news, though, didn't cause great rejoicing in the country. A closer look into Albert's background showed that his kingdoms of Coburg and Goth combined were roughly the size of Dorset. Their annual revenue was a measly £128,000. Added to this, many of Victoria's stuck-up subjects had no time for Germans. They held the view that all Germans were poor, dirty and, even worse, pipe-smokers! Albert was regarded as a beggar who was no fit match for Victoria. Popular songs of the day were very rude about him:

Parliament wasn't any more welcoming to poor Albert than the public. When an allowance of £50,000 a year was proposed, they voted to cut it to a mere £30,000.

Albert suffered at his wife's hands too. Victoria wouldn't let him choose his own private secretary or the gentlemen to wait on him. When he wanted a longer honeymoon than the two or three days she proposed, she replied in a letter:

> *You forget, my dearest Love, that I am the Sovereign and that business can stop and wait for nothing.*

Victoria was used to getting her way and it was clear she was going to wear the trousers in the marriage. However, Albert was no pet poodle. He'd lost round one to Victoria but there was always round two after the wedding.

THE HARD TIMES

10th February 1840

QUEEN WEDS HER ALBERT

The young Queen married Prince Albert at St James's Palace today. Thousands gathered on the route to see the bride, some climbing – and falling – out of trees. Victoria usually brings her own sunny weather, but on this occasion she failed miserably.

The Queen looked a vision of splendour in a white satin dress and diamond necklace. Prince Albert wore the uniform of a British Field-Marshal (let's hope he gave it back after the service). The wedding cake weighed 300 pounds and was nine feet wide. It needs to be big since pieces will be sent all over the world. Guests were surprised to hear Victoria promise to obey her husband during the marriage vows. Bets are being taken on how long that will last!

Bloomers and bustles

At her wedding, Victoria wore a white satin gown, trimmed with lace. State occasions with balls and banquets meant that Victoria had to take an interest in fashion. Her favourite colour was pink which showed off her diamonds so well. Sometimes, however, she plumped for brighter colours. Once, when visiting France, she carried a handbag embroidered with a parrot and wore a dress covered in red geraniums. The fashionable French thought that she looked like a walking flower shop! Once she was married, Victoria always asked Albert's advice on what to wear. (Not a good idea since Albert didn't exactly dress in the height of fashion himself.) Fashion changed a great deal during Victoria's reign. Here are some of the crazes that came and went.

Top ten Victorian fashions

1 The hoopskirt

Skirts got wider and wider during Victoria's reign, reaching a record ten metres around and causing the wearer to get stuck in doors and turnstiles. The hoopskirt was the brainchild of the English designer Charles Worth, who invented it to hide the French Empress Eugenie's bulging tum when she was pregnant.

2 The bustle

By the 1870s women had got tired of looking like circus tents. The hoopskirt was replaced by the bustle which put all the padding behind the wearer. A variation on the bustle was the crenelate – so wide it was said that you could balance a tea-tray on it.

3 The Albert waistcoat

Not to be outshone by women in the fashion stakes, Albert gave his name to the double-breasted waistcoat.

4 The cardigan

Lord Cardigan, a famous Victorian, was warming himself with his back to the fire one night. Unfortunately he got too close and burnt his coat tails. Undismayed, Cardigan cut them off and with one snip invented the casual short jacket. It came to be known as the cardigan.

5 Muttonchops and Piccadilly weepers

During the Crimean War shaving was a problem so the officers grew beards. This quickly caught on back home. Young men grew facial fungus to make them look older and more reliable. Later on beards got the chop and were replaced by enormous side whiskers known as muttonchops or Piccadilly weepers.

6 The blooming bloomer

Mrs Amelia Bloomer, an American, caused a scandal in 1851 by promoting baggy trousers for women. The trousers were worn under a knee-length skirt and were soon mockingly nicknamed 'bloomers' . They were much more practical but Victorians found women wearing trousers shocking and Mrs Bloomer was accused of being a marriage wrecker. In Victorian society men wore the trousers and women were meant to be fragile and obedient. (Victoria was an exception, of course.)

7 The suspender

In 1876 a greater scandal than the bloomer hit London. The Grand Opera Bouffe appeared at the Alhambra Theatre and the audience were shocked to see French dancers with 'naked thighs with suspenders stretched across them to keep up the stockings.' Up to now most women had to wear garters to keep their stockings from falling down, now the twangy suspender took over.

8 Big drawers

By the 1880s luxury undies were being made in soft silk and lace. The Victorians liked their knickers big. Linen drawers were so enormous that there was room for three or four people inside. By the end of the century drawers were being challenged by *combinations* which combined pants and vest into one undie.

9 Corsets

Women were supposed to have slim waists, so slim that their husbands could reach right round them with their hands. In order to achieve this women spent hours being laced into stiff whalebone corsets. Sometimes these were so tight that women couldn't breathe and fainted. Some even went so far as having their bottom ribs removed in the interests of fashion. Victoria herself was warned against getting too fat and advised to go for walks. She declined on the grounds that she might get stones in her shoes. 'Get tighter shoes,' was Lord Melbourne's reply.

10 Raging purple

In 1856 purple became all the rage when W H Perkin discovered that a new bright purple dye could be made from coal-tar. Soon everyone was wearing purple hats, dresses, gloves and hats. One writer commented: 'We shall soon have purple omnibuses and purple houses.'

Five years later Victoria would make black all the rage when she went into 13 years of mourning. For now she was delighted with married life. Albert and Victoria settled down to a family life of perfect contentment. Most of the time.

TIMELINE: VICTORIA AND ALBERT

1855: DAVID LIVINGSTONE STUMBLES ON A BIG WATERFALL IN AFRICA AND CALLS IT THE VICTORIA FALLS.
THAT SHOULD BE ENOUGH FOR A KNIGHTHOOD!
1856: VICTORIA CROSS MEDAL INTRODUCED FOR BRAVERY.
OUCH!
BE BRAVE...
1857: INDIAN MUTINY - THE SEPOYS ARE REVOLTING
COME HERE AND SAY THAT!
1859: DARWIN'S THEORY OF EVOLUTION CLAIMS MONKEYS AND HUMANS ARE RELATED.
DARWIN'S BOOK UNFAIR TO APES
1861: DARLING ALBERT DIES OF TYPHOID FEVER. VICTORIA GOES INTO MOURNING - FOR THE NEXT 13 YEARS!
THERE, THERE! YOU'LL SOON GET OVER IT!

'WE ARE A FAMILY' - AT HOME WITH ALBERT

He is an angel . . . To look in those dear eyes and that dear sunny face is enough to make me adore him.

Victoria was so delighted with her husband that she often had to check he hadn't sprouted wings and a halo. Prince Albert was not only good-looking but brainy. At 21 he seemed much older than Victoria (though he was the same age). Albert had come to Britain hoping to make himself useful in public life. However, Victoria warned him that the British didn't like foreigners interfering in their affairs and he had better keep his nose out. Poor Albert found himself kicking his heels with nothing to do.

In the early days of their courtship, Albert stood by Victoria while she signed her state papers.

The paper Prince was there to support Victoria and help her bear royal babies. Apart from that he wasn't to be allowed to meddle. This became clear from the start when the question of Albert's title was raised. What should he be called?

Victoria wanted him to be called King Consort but Melbourne rejected this on the grounds that once the English started making kings they'd soon start *unmaking* them. Albert had to make do with his own title, Prince Albert of Saxe-Coburg. Eventually Victoria insisted he be given the title Prince Consort. This didn't help settle the matter of a role for the royal husband. Parliament decreed he was to have no power in politics, no rank in the army and no place in the House of Lords. What was a young prince with brains and energy to do with himself?

Who wears the trousers?

At home, Victoria didn't easily forget that she was queen. Albert was well aware that in most homes the husband was the lord and master. But then most husbands weren't married to the Queen of England.

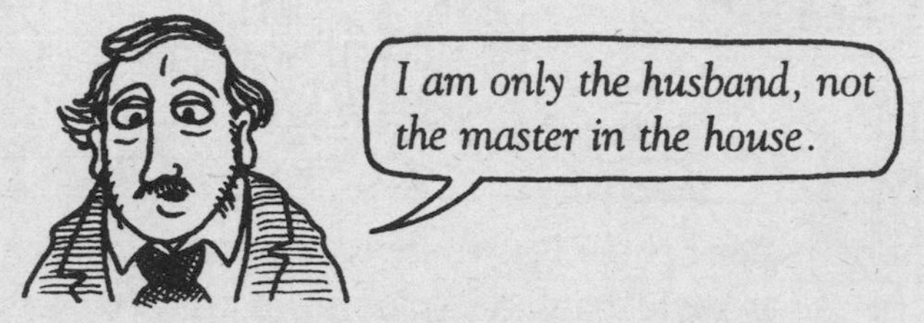

This led to occasional quarrels. Victoria loved her dear Albert, but she could sometimes be proud and bossy. Once, she drove Albert so mad that he walked out and locked himself in his private apartments. Victoria knocked on the door but Albert wouldn't open it until she answered. Their argument sounds like one of those old knock knock jokes:

From the start Albert was given a desk next to Victoria's, but he had nothing to do except talk to his wife or write letters.

Victoria was still liable to lose her temper and fly into a rage, so there was no sense in fighting her for power. Albert saw that his best bet was to wait and be patient. Things began to change when Victoria became pregnant for the first time. Then the Queen started to rely on Albert more and more to take care of state business for her. In time she began to rely on his advice in everything, especially since all her ministers praised his good sense. Albert had slipped off his leash – and he'd only just begun.

The frog princes

Obviously one of the main reasons royals get married is to have children. A childless king or a queen is like a firework in the rain – they're going to fizzle out sooner or later. (No one guessed that Victoria was going to hang around for another 60 years.)

Unfortunately, having babies was one of the things Victoria hated doing. She wasn't at all pleased when she got pregnant and dreaded the whole business of childbirth. She could be sentimental about animals – sobbing herself to sleep when Albert's favourite wolfhound died – but she couldn't stand babies in what she called 'the frog stage'.

Having them was one thing, but breast-feeding them was quite another. Once when she saw her daughter Alice breast-feeding, she ordered that a cow in the royal dairy be called Princess Alice.

In later life when Princess Victoria (our Vicky's daughter) became pregnant and wrote of the wonder of giving birth to an 'immortal soul', her mother replied dryly: 'I think much more of our being like an animal, I felt more like a cow or a dog at such moments.'

Victoria felt the first two years of her married life were utterly spoiled by having a baby. Still after the first one she went on to have eight more. Naturally Vicky's kids weren't just there to fill the nursery. Through them she became the Grandmother of Europe with royal relatives everywhere.

Victoria's nine babies were born at the rate of one every two years, so it's hardly surprising if she looked fat and frumpy in old age. With their fast growing family,

Victoria and Albert settled down to home life, showing the nation a model of domestic bliss. Actually it wasn't always like that. With Albert's strong views and Victoria's temper tantrums, storms were inevitable.

One erupted over the health of Princess Victoria, their first child. When the child grew sickly, the Queen's doctor, Sir James Clark, failed to make her better. Albert thought Clark was a bungler and the Queen was to blame. He wrote her a note:

Dr Clark has mismanaged the child and poisoned her with calomel and you have starved her. I shall have nothing more to do with it; take the child away and do as you like and if she dies you will have it on your conscience.

Victoria, stubborn as ever, wouldn't give in and – not for the first time – Albert's old tutor, Baron Stockmar had to act as the peace-maker.

As it turned out, Albert was probably right about Clark. Later the bungling doctor would cost him his life.

When the Princess Royal was three months old a curious rumour went round that she'd been born blind and without any feet. People love to hear bad news about royalty and the rumour proved hard to quell. When the court artist C R Leslie showed a sketch of the Princess at a party he was told: 'What a pity so fine a child should be entirely blind.' In vain, Leslie protested that the royal sprog's eyes were bright and she took notice of everything around her. No one would believe him. Though her eyes might be bright it was *certain* that she was blind.

'HOW WE LAUGHED' – Queen Victoria was amused

At a dinner party, Victoria once described how her mother, the Duchess of Kent, once carried a fork out of the dining room after dinner. The old lady's eyesight wasn't so good and she'd mistaken it for her fan.

At another dinner party the Queen told with roars of laughter how shocked her Master of the Household had been by a design for some important medals. . .

Jobs for Albert

While Victoria got on with providing an heir to the throne, Albert was at last finding scope for his talents. His first job was to put his house in order. In Albert's case the house was Buckingham Palace (and Windsor Castle) and the accounts were in a mess. On investigation, Albert discovered that all sorts of sharp practices were going on under the Queen's nose. In her palaces, hundreds of candles were put in chandeliers daily[1] and then disposed of, whether they'd been used or not. Where did the candles go? The servants sold them off for pocket money as 'Palace ends'.

Tradesman brought goods that were never seen in Buckingham Palace and many officials were stuffing themselves on the Queen's charity. Meanwhile the captain who had stood guard over George III still got an annual wine allowance of 35 shillings from the Queen!

Albert blamed Victoria's old governess Lehzen for the household's hopeless chaos. It wasn't only the accounts that were in a mess, he soon discovered that security in the Palace was a shambles. How did he know? One day he found an intruder sleeping under a sofa. Here's how a Victorian police officer might have reported the outrage.

Police Report, 2nd December 1840
Arresting Officer: PC Peeler

Shortly after 1 a.m. the nurse reported she heard a suspicious noise in the Queen's sitting room. Calling a page to investigate, they apprehended a boy asleep under a sofa. The intruder was identified as one Edmund Jones, 17-year-old son of a tailor, who had been seen in the Palace on a previous occasion.

1 Buckingham Palace didn't get gas lights until 1846 – some 40 years after the first in London.

On being questioned the suspect alleged he could gain entrance to the Palace any time he liked 'by shinning over a wall and bunking through a window'. When asked why he'd entered Her Majesty's apartment he replied: 'I wanted to know how the Queen and such live at the Palace. I thought it'd look nice in a book one day.' He claimed to have sat on the throne, seen the Queen herself and heard the little Princess 'squalling'.

Further investigation in the Palace kitchens revealed that the intruder had also helped himself to various eatables during the night. On arrest, Master Jones put on an air of great dignity and requested me to 'behave to him as I ought to a gentleman who is likely to rise high in the world'.

'Boy Jones' was arrested three times for breaking and entering the Palace. The first time it happened he was declared mad. The second time he was sentenced to three months on the treadmill in the House of Correction. Finally, when he went back a third time, he was sent to sea. Sadly, the only way he rose high in the world was probably by climbing the rigging. Albert meanwhile blew his top at the lack of safety for his family.

The Boy Jones wasn't thc only scare that Victoria had to endure. During her first pregnancy there was an attempt to kill her.

THE HARD TIMES

10th June 1840

MADMAN ATTACKS QUEEN

The Queen came within inches of death today when she was shot at not once but twice only a 100 yards from her home. The Queen was out driving in her open carriage with Prince Albert, when a sinister assassin appeared from nowhere and took a potshot from six paces. The Queen only survived because he was a rotten shot. The pistol crack frightened the horses and stopped them in their tracks.

The Prince recalled: 'He was a little mean-looking man, standing with his arms crossed and a pistol in each hand. His attitude was so theatrical it amused me.'

The Prince wasn't laughing though when the madman took aim a second time. Thanks to Albert's quick action the Queen ducked down out of sight. Shortly after, the gunman – Edward Oxford, a waiter – was arrested.

Waiter- brought to order

The cool reactions of the Queen and her Consort have been praised by many. They are applauded in the streets and choruses of 'God Save the Queen' ring out wherever they go.

It was the first attempt to kill the Queen but not the last. During her long reign Victoria suffered a staggering *seven* assassination attempts.

Home sweet palace

Away from the public eye what did Victoria and Albert actually do with themselves?

In a typical day at the Palace, mornings were taken up with work – Albert by now drafting letters for Victoria and reading all state papers.

After lunch there might be some play-time – the royal couple playing piano duets together or sketching portraits. In public, Albert was serious and solemn, but with his children he was different. He was often found playing on the floor with young Bertie and Pussy (that's Princess Vicky, not the cat).

Dinner was a more solemn affair. The only time Albert came alive was when discussing thrilling topics such as drainage or heating. The Gentlemen and Ladies in Waiting were present but weren't allowed to go to bed until the Queen yawned politely and retired. This was rarely after ten o'clock. After dinner Albert would take himself off to play a game of chess. Sometimes Victoria would have to send a servant to remind him that it was past his bedtime. Who was he playing in these absorbing chess matches? Himself!

Albert lights up Christmas

Christmas was one of Victoria's favourite times. Christmas was usually at Windsor Castle and celebrated in the German style. Albert introduced his family to the German custom of the Christmas tree. One tree wasn't enough though, each member of the royal family got their own small Christmas tree decorated with candles, sweetmeats and cakes hung from ribbons. Actually Christmas trees had been imported earlier in the century, but it was Albert's example that led to the fashion catching on. Endlessly talked about in the new illustrated papers, the Royal Family Christmas was a public event. Soon families all over England were stacking their brightly wrapped presents under the Christmas tree. (Except poor families who didn't have any trees or presents to put under them.)

In the winter Albert also enjoyed the outdoor sports of tobogganing, building snowmen and ice-skating. Once, in a nasty accident, skating was nearly the death of him.

VICTORIA'S SECRET DIARY

12th February 1841

Day very cold but bright. Dear Albert wanted to go ice-skating on the pond at the Palace and this nearly led to a most dreadful tragedy. I warned him to be careful but he would go.

What a blessing that I accompanied him to the pond with Lady Palmerston, though intending only to watch. He had hardly set foot on the ice when it cracked and started to break up. I cannot convey my feelings of dread as I saw my poor darling fall and sink! For a moment his dear head disappeared below the black icy water. I thought he was lost to me for ever. Lady Palmerston was screaming (a fat help she was). Then

Albert bobbed up, gasping for air, and I was able to reach out my hand and pull him to safety.

Heaven be blessed for preserving his life! What a mercy that Albert can swim! I hope he'll never, never scare me like this again. (I've hidden his skates where he won't find them.)

'HOW WE LAUGHED' -Queen Victoria was amused

In the summer, Victoria enjoyed trips to the seaside. During the Victorian age, doctors recommended sea bathing as good for your health. Seaside resorts such as Brighton became fashionable for the upper classes as well as the poor. However, bathing was a problem. The glimpse of a woman's leg was considered shocking by the Victorians (even table legs had to be covered up). Swimming costumes were neck to toe affairs and taking a dip wasn't a simple matter. Victoria had her first sea bathe in 1847 at Osborne on the Isle of Wight.

After that first experience, Victoria changed her routine. She would delicately sponge her face with water before going into the sea, then 'plunge about' in the water, making sure she kept her head upright. We can safely say that Victoria wasn't a strong swimmer.

Educating Bertie

Meanwhile, Victoria's large family was growing up and that brought new worries. Out of her nine children, all her hopes for the future were pinned on Albert Edward – better known as Bertie. It was Bertie who would be her successor one day. From an early age Albert and Victoria set out to educate their eldest son as the future King of Britain.

I wish that he should grow up entirely under his father's eye, and every step be guided by him.

Victoria really wanted her son to be a miniature Albert. The trouble was that Bertie wasn't brainy like his papa, he was a bit dim. No end of tutors or lessons could discover brains where there weren't any. Princess Victoria, Bertie's eldest sister, was clever and strong, but the Queen often remarked that Bertie was a stupid boy.

From an early age Bertie's only talents seemed to be charm and chasing women. Once, as a child, Victoria overheard Bertie telling Lady Beauvale how he had nearly fallen overboard on a cruise. The Queen sent him off with a flea in his ear for telling lies.

Bertie's tutor from the age of seven, was the Reverend Henry Birch who drew up a strict timetable of six-and-a-half hours a day studying English, Writing, French, Maths, Music, German, Drawing and Geography. There was no room for play or sport on the menu. No room for girls either, which may be why they were Bertie's favourite sport in later life. Bertie's miserable day began and ended with prayers recited in front of his tutor. He hated it. His lessons bored him and he took to making faces, spitting and even throwing stones at his tutors. When his German tutor tried to tell him off, Bertie really got angry.

Bertie's parents never understood him. By trying to turn him into his upright, clever father, Victoria only succeeded in achieving exactly the opposite. Bertie grew into a fat, foolish prince who was the black sheep of the family. Yet maybe if Victoria had shown him a bit more kindness and affection as a child, he might have turned out differently.

While Bertie was growing up and behaving badly, his parents were determined to do their duty for the country. Albert, especially, had ideas in his head that would force the country to admit he was a pretty clever chap after all.

'WE ARE DOING OUR DUTY' – VICTORIA AT WORK

Albert had a dream. He wanted to organize an exhibition. Not a little show of his sketches, but something on a much grander scale. In the mid-19th century he felt that society had entered a wonderful period of progress and invention that would create a better world. (Albert was a great optimist.)

Many people thought the Prince should be put in a strait-jacket and led quietly away to the nearest padded cell. But Albert hadn't lost his marbles. His dream was to put on the greatest trade show the world had ever seen. It would be a giant shop-window for Britain's arts, crafts and industries. Not only that, it would provide a stage for the best exhibits from all over the world. The Great Exhibition was the Millennium Dome of its day – and it had just as much trouble getting off the ground.

Albert's great greenhouse

Naturally many people pooh-poohed the idea from the start. (They hadn't forgotten that Albert wasn't even British, dammit.) Parliament was among the party-poopers, refusing to vote any money to Albert's grand scheme. But Victoria backed her husband with a gift of £1,000 and once the Queen took the lead, other donations soon followed.

The big question was where to hold it. Albert needed a big space for his Exhibition and Hyde Park in London was the obvious choice. *The Times* newspaper protested that it would turn the park into a magnet for all the 'vagabonds' in London (meaning the pongy poor who the upper classes preferred not to see). Even worse, said the whingeing critics, a huge brick monstrosity would ruin the look of the park.

Luckily for Albert he found a man who could solve his problem. The architect Joseph Paxton suggested building a glass and iron structure that would be big enough to cover the trees of Hyde Park. It could be assembled piece by piece and taken down afterwards so the Park wouldn't have to be spoiled. The Crystal Palace – as it was soon nicknamed – would be the wonder of the century. Albert's Great Greenhouse Show was up and running.

The Great Exhibition was opened on May day of 1851. Twenty-five thousand guests were invited to the ceremony and watched the Queen – dressed in pink and glowing with pride – declare the show open to a peal of the Hallelujah Chorus.

The doom-merchants had to admit that they were wrong. Albert's Great Greenhouse Show was a sparkling success. Throughout the summer an average of 60,000 people a day streamed into the Exhibition hall, marvelling at the wonders inside. Many had claimed the glass palace would collapse like a pack of cards in a gale. Others said that the roof would offer a giant bullseye for

passing sparrows and the weight of their droppings would shatter the glass. ('Sparrow hawks,' suggested the Duke of Wellington when the problem was put to him.) Every problem and difficulty was brought personally to Albert who worked day and night. 'My poor Albert is terribly fagged,' wrote Victoria in her diary. ('Fagged' meant tired in Victorian slang.)

Yet, in the end, it was all worth it. The sun shone on the opening day and Victoria rode in her carriage through streets packed with cheering people. It was, wrote Victoria, the greatest day of her life. (Although it's true she'd said that before.)

The tremendous cheering, the joy expressed in every face, the vastness of the building with all its decorations and exhibits, the sound of the organ, and my beloved husband the creator of this great 'Peace festival' . . . all this was indeed moving and a day to live for ever.

REAL DIARY EXTRACT

Naturally the grand opening day didn't pass entirely without a hitch. In the procession a man in full Chinese dress was spotted walking proudly between the Archbishop of Canterbury and the Duke of Wellington. It was assumed he was an important ambassador from China and it was a bit embarrassing when it was later discovered that he was the owner of a junk-boat moored on the Thames.

'HOW WE LAUGHED'
~ Queen Victoria was amused

An embarrassing blunder happened when the Queen began her tour and stooped to admire one of the stalls showing engraved glass. The Queen pointed to a glass which showed a boy jumping from a boat while a giant eye watched him from the clouds. The flustered craftsman explained:

'The boy, Madam, is the Prince of Wales, and the eye is the eye of God looking out with pleasure for the moment when his Royal Highness will land on his kingdom and become the reigning sovereign.' There was an appalled silence. Was the man suggesting it would be a happy day when the Queen popped her clogs? Victoria moved on until she'd passed the stall; then she burst out laughing.

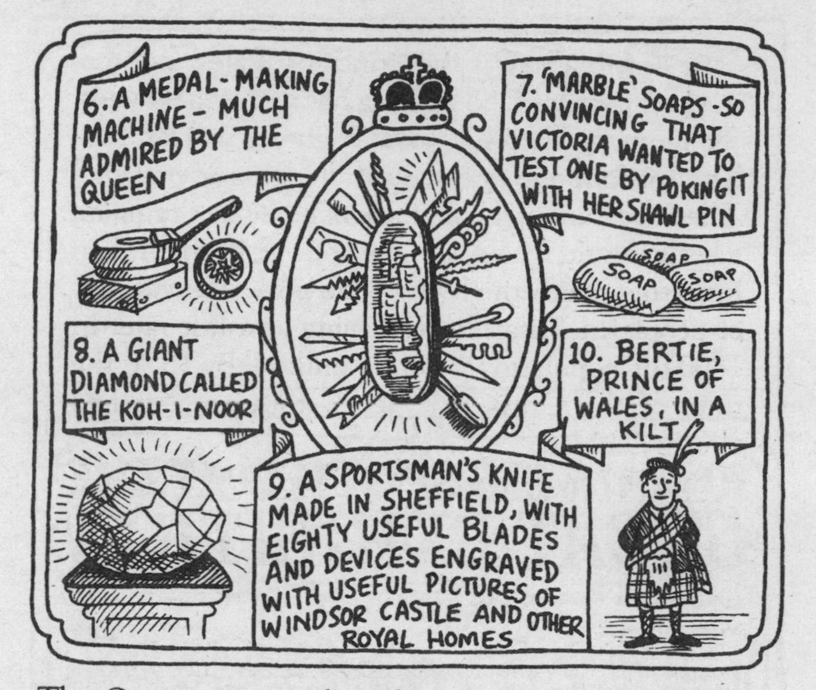

The Queen was so pleased with the Great Exhibition that she visited almost every day. Her Majesty wasn't the only enthusiast. In all, six million visitors came – that was *one in three* of the population of England and Wales. Today it's hard to imagine anything that could draw such a massive audience. (Unless the National Lottery started giving prizes for attending the draw.)

The new railways brought people from the north who had never seen a train before, let alone set eyes on London. The papers predicted that riots would break out in the streets if the Exhibition let in the pongy poor. As it turned out no one pinched the Koh-i-noor diamond or even picked a tulip from the park. The sight of the working class behaving as well as their betters was hailed as the greatest marvel of all.

The stinky poor

Albert's dream of the new age of invention bringing a better world for all was a nice thought, but it had little to do with the lives of the poor. The number of people in Britain was growing at a fast rate. In 1800 the population was 15.5 million. By 1851, the time of the Great Exhibition, that number had almost doubled.

In 1800 most people lived and worked in the countryside. By 1850 millions had moved into the towns and cities, looking for work. Britain's Industrial Revolution was built on coal, machinery and cheap labour. Parts of the Midlands became known as the Black Country because everything was black – from the smoke-belching chimneys to the grubby faces of the miserable workers.

In the cities, poor families were crammed into dirty slums. In parts of London as many as 40 people lived in one terraced house. And they were the lucky ones! Homeless people could pay for 'a penny hang' – a space on a thick rope over which you hung and tried to get some sleep.

The Great Stink

Cities were often filled with rubbish, and human waste was carried away by 'nightsoil men'. The sewers of London were said to contain: dead dogs and cats, huge rats, rotten fish, slime, rags and stable dung. No wonder Londoners covered themselves in perfume.

Sometimes the sewage seeped into the rivers. Even the Queen wasn't safe – pongy poo from the Thames occasionally turned up in her garden at Windsor castle. It was good for the roses but Victoria had it chucked back in the river.

Things reached a whiffy peak in 1858 – known as the year of 'The Great Stink'. It was a long hot summer and the revolting stench from the Thames got so bad that many MPs were sick. Parliament had to be closed while a group of brave MPs were volunteered to find a solution. They suggested a fund to raise money for a new drainage system under London.

'HOW WE LAUGHED' - Queen Victoria was amused

Victoria was once shown round Trinity College, Cambridge, with Albert who had just been awarded an honorary degree. At the time Cambridge's sewage system was as bad as London's and all the poo and paper went into the river. As the royal party stopped on a bridge, the Queen pointed down at the water and asked, 'What are all those pieces of paper floating down the river?' It was a delicate moment but the Master of Trinity rose to the occasion.

Whigs and big hats

The triumph of the Great Exhibition was Albert's, although Victoria bathed in her fair share of the glory. Much of her daily routine was taken up by politics and meeting with her Prime Ministers. Victoria must have had trouble remembering their names since there were ten of them in all. Her first Prime Minister in 1838 was Lord Melbourne, her last one would be Lord Salisbury in 1901.

Hairy Victorian Prime Ministers

Name	Party	Number of goes as Prime Minister
Lord Melbourne	Whig	1
Sir Robert Peel	Tory	1
Lord John Russell	Whig	2
Earl of Derby	Tory	3
Earl of Aberdeen	Tory	1
Lord Palmerston	Whig	1
Benjamin Disraeli	Tory	2
William Gladstone	Whig	4
Marquis of Salisbury	Tory	2
Earl of Rosebury	Whig	1

Victorian politics was fought between two parties – Whigs and Tories. A third party also emerged late in Victoria's reign – the Labour Party – but at first they only had one MP. His name was Keir Hardie and to show his working-class roots he turned up at Parliament in a dirty working suit, cloth cap and followed by a noisy brass band.

How could you tell the Whigs from the Tories? Sadly the Whigs didn't sport silly wigs to identify themselves. Both Whig and Tory MPs preferred hairy sidewhiskers and big top hats.

Victoria herself was a staunch Whig supporter when she first became Queen, but that was only because all her pals, including Lord Melbourne, were Whigs.

Albert taught her the wisdom of a queen not taking sides in politics, but at heart she was really a Tory, especially in later life. Here's a guide to the most famous of Victoria's ten Prime Ministers.

KNOW YOUR

ROBERT PEEL
Tory Prime Minister
(twice: 1834–5, 1841–6)

Royal relations: *Awkward, tended to shuffle his feet. But Albert was a big fan.*
Finest hour: *Created the police force (nicknamed Peelers). Abolished Corn Laws so the poor could buy bread.*
Victoria's verdict: *'She would like him better if he could keep his legs still.' – as reported by Lord Greville.*

LORD PALMERSTON
Whig Prime Minister
(twice: 1855–8, 1859–65)

Royal relations – *Stormy. V and A referred to his frequent blunders as 'bocks'.*
Finest hour: *Once made a speech lasting nearly five hours defending his foreign policy.*
Victoria's verdict: *'He had often worried and distressed us.'*

PRIME MINISTERS

BENJAMIN DISRAELI

Also known as: Dizzy / the Earl of Beaconsfield

Tory Prime Minister (twice: 1868, 1874–80)

Royal relations: *Warm. 'Flattery will you get you everywhere, Prime Minister.'*

Finest hour: *Doubled the number of voters, made Victoria Empress of India.*

Victoria's verdict: *'He is full of poetry, romance and chivalry.'*

WILLIAM GLADSTONE

Also known as: the Grand Old Man (G.O.M.)

Whig Prime Minister (four times: 1868–74, 1880–5, 1886, 1892–4)

Royal relations: *Frosty. He talked to Victoria as if he was giving a public lecture.*

Finest hour: *Sat in Parliament for 61 years (until died of boredom).*

Victoria's verdict: *'The abominable G man.'*

Dizzy versus the Grand Old Man

The two great political giants of Victoria's reign were as different as chalk and cheese. Gladstone and Disraeli frequently clashed in Parliament where cool, debonair Dizzy had the advantage over his irritable opponent.

William Ewart Gladstone was a deeply religious man, who thought that God's will and his own plans were pretty much the same thing. So devout was Gladstone that he spent his free time prowling the back-streets, finding 'ladies of the night' to talk to. Gladstone said he wasn't interested in their bodies, it was their souls he was trying to save. Knowing Gladstone it was probably true, but think what Queen Victoria would have made of his hobby if she had known. (Lucky for Gladstone that the tabloid press hadn't been invented!)

Victoria thought Gladstone was a total crackpot. He had none of Disraeli's wit and charm, and always made the mistake of lecturing the Queen rather than flattering her. Gladstone once arrived late to see Victoria and only made matters worse by trying to pass it off with a weak joke. He had three hands he told the queen, 'a left hand, a right hand and a little behindhand.'

'We are not amused,' replied the stony-faced Queen in her famous phrase.

In contrast to glum Gladstone, Disraeli was one of the most flamboyant Prime Ministers Britain has ever had. The son of a Spanish Jew, Disraeli was baptized a Christian as a boy. He was a complete outsider in an age where most MPs were blue-blooded Englishman. Disraeli's weapons were his wit and his charm. In his spare time he was a popular novelist. 'If I want to read a good novel I write one!' he said modestly.

Dizzy liked to cut a dash in the Commons and wore jewelled rings, fancy waistcoats and a goatee beard. He also dyed his hair when it became grey. Although Victoria at first thought he was a bounder she grew to like him. This was because Dizzy knew the best way of pleasing the Queen – by crawling to her shamelessly.

It's said a woman once sat next to Gladstone at dinner one night, and next to Dizzy the next. Asked for her opinion on the two great men she said: 'When I left the dining-room after sitting next to Gladstone I thought he was the cleverest man in England. But after sitting next to Mr Disraeli I thought I was the cleverest woman in England.' Victoria probably felt much the same and that's why she always preferred Disraeli.

Travelling first class

Away from politics, Victoria spent much of her time moving between her various homes at Buckingham Palace, Windsor Castle, Balmoral in Scotland and Osborne House on the Isle of Wight. Travelling from London to Scotland could have been a long uncomfortable business but luckily for Victoria train travel had arrived by the beginning of her reign.

Before trains most people got about by horse-drawn coaches which were noisy, bumpy and painfully slow. In London you were likely to be held up by the crowds or a wandering sheep crossing the road. There was no highway code, so accidents and disputes were routine affairs. Trains soon caught on since they were lightning fast in comparison. A four-day coach journey from London to York took only 12 hours by train. The first public steam railway line opened in 1825 and by the 1840s even Victoria was letting the train take the strain.

We arrived here yesterday morning, having come by the railroad from Windsor, in half an hour, free from dust and crowd and heat, and I am quite charmed by it.

REAL DIARY EXTRACT

Of course Victoria's experience of rail-travel wasn't quite like her subjects. She had her own private carriage upholstered in royal blue silk, with padded walls and ceiling to deaden the noise and vibration. Albert and

Victoria even had two brass beds in their carriage so that they could snooze their way through the journey.

Life was very different for a servant who travelled in third class. They were lucky to get a seat on a wooden bench. The sides of the coach were so low that passengers often fell out on the journey! To make matters worse most carriages had no roof, leaving the passengers to get drenched to the skin in bad weather. Dry days weren't much better. Passengers were blackened with cinders from the engine or choked with smoke when the train entered a tunnel. Funny that train travel was so popular.

Ruling the waves

When at sea the Queen had a private paddle-wheeled steam-yacht called the *Victoria and Albert* (no surprises there). The 1,000-ton steamer was ordered by the Admiralty (and paid for by the nation) in 1843.

Steamships were starting to take over from sailing ships in the mid-19th century and in 1858 a monster steamer, the *Great Western*, was launched. Designed by the famous engineer, Isambard Kingdom Brunel (we'll meet him later), the ship was six times as big as any other ship on the ocean.

Steamships would go on getting bigger and bigger until the launch of the 'unsinkable' liner, the *Titanic*. It sank in 1912.

Country life

As we've mentioned, Victoria didn't spend all her time in Buckingham Palace. She had a whole collection of royal residences to choose from. The Queen preferred Windsor Castle to Buck House, but Albert was more of a country boy at heart. (No wonder, with all the stinks getting up his nose in the city.)

Victoria and Albert soon looked around for a humble country house they could retreat to with their family. They found two – Balmoral in Scotland and Osborne House on the Isle of Wight, which clever Albert had rebuilt to his own design. For the royal couple these two houses offered peaceful oases away from court life. They weren't so popular with ministers who had to make the long train journey from Westminster to see the Queen.

The Royal Piles

Buckingham Palace

Bought by Victoria's grandfather, George III, for a snip in 1762, Buck House was a regular choice for state banquets. Albert had the builders in to add a balcony to the front and do something about the pongy drains and toilets.

Victoria's verdict: Fond of the Palace and London life, till Albert arrived. He preferred the country hidey-holes of Osborne and Balmoral.

Osborne House

Seaside holiday home designed and built by Albert in Italian style. Albert bought it with Victoria's private money and the sale of Brighton Pavilion. He organized the planting of the garden by standing on a high platform and using a system of flag signals to show where to plant the trees. The children had their own Swiss cottage and a fort where the boys played soldiers.

Victoria's verdict: 'It is impossible to imagine a prettier spot. . . We can walk about anywhere without being followed or mobbed.' (At Brighton she'd complained that children stared at her as if she was a brass band.)

Balmoral

Victoria's Scottish hidey hole which she bought with money left to her by an eccentric miser, John Camden Nield. The mountains and forests reminded Albert of Germany, and later the place reminded Victoria of her dear departed Albert. At Balmoral, Victoria let her peasant dreams run wild. She enjoyed porridge for breakfast, the wail of the bagpipes, the clean air and the Highland dancing. The Ghillies' (servants') balls were wild drunken affairs in which Victoria sometimes joined in the hooligan (it's a dance). The royals even took to wearing kilts themselves.

Victoria's verdict: 'A pretty little castle.'

Windsor Castle

The oldest royal pile in Britain and the world's largest inhabited castle. Windsor was begun by William the Conqueror in 1066 and improved by successive monarchs. Twenty-year-old Victoria met her Albert and fell in love at Windsor. The smell from the Thames was the only drawback of Windsor. Albert once discovered the 53 cesspools (underground pits where the loos drained) were overflowing. Part of Windsor Castle had to close because of the rotten stench.

Victoria's verdict: Spent her three-day honeymoon at the old castle. Who needs the south of France when you've got Windsor?

What Victoria and Albert liked more than anything was a quiet home life. Victorians thought of their home as their castle – and Victoria was no exception. (Well, her home *was* a castle.) Countless Victorian magazines were devoted to the happiness of home and the daily pleasures of family life. The Queen's own pleasures were simple ones. Here she is describing a typical evening at home at Osborne in 1844.

> *The children again with us, & such a pleasure & interest. Bertie & Alice are the greatest friends & always playing together. Later we both read to each other. When I read I sit on a sofa in the middle of the room . . . Albert sitting in a low armchair . . . with another small table in front of him on which he usually stands his book. Oh, if I could only describe our dear happy life together!*
>
> REAL DIARY EXTRACT

Not exactly thrilling but Victoria was happy. She had no idea that her happiness with Albert wasn't going to last. Before long Albert would be gone – a victim of the stinky drains at Windsor which spread disease. For Victoria, losing her darling Albert would be the beginning of the Great Misery. It wasn't too much fun for her subjects either.

TIMELINE: VICTORIA ALONE

1884: ANOTHER YEAR, ANOTHER FUNERAL. VICTORIA'S SON LEOPOLD DIES.
ERK!
NOT AGAIN!
1887: 50 YEARS ON THE THRONE. VICTORIA'S GOLDEN JUBILEE PARTY.
WHOOPEE
1897: DIAMOND JUBILEE. 60, NOT OUT.
SIGH...
1899: BOER WAR BREAKS OUT. VICTORIA SENDS CHOCOLATE.
FANCY A MARS BOER?
1900: GOOD GRIEF! VICTORIA'S SON ALFRED DIES.
NOT AGAIN AGAIN!
ARG!
1901: VICTORIA GIVES UP THE GHOST AT 81. BERTIE FINALLY BECOMES KING EDWARD VII.

'WE ARE IN MOURNING' - DEAD ALBERT LIVES

Victoria had always been stronger than Albert. She was rarely ill and disliked warm rooms. Seeing a fire lit in a room, the Queen would order it to be put out to the annoyance of her shivering guests. Albert, in contrast, often complained of the cold and sometimes took unusual measures to keep his head warm.

He was overworked and worried by the scrapes his son, bad Bertie, was getting into. Yet when the Prince died, at the age of only 42 years old, it was a great shock to everyone, especially Victoria.

THE HARD TIMES

15th December 1861

ALBERT DEAD – DOCTORS BUNGLED

Prince Albert died late yesterday evening. It's said that the Prince died of typhoid fever – a result of the rotten drains at Windsor. But some are saying that his life might have been saved by a decent doctor.

Albert's doctor was Sir James Clark – the Queen's old favourite. 'Old' is the word since Sir James is 73 and was assisted by the equally doddery Sir Henry Holland. These two, Lord Clarendon claimed, 'had not been fit to attend a sick cat.'

Sir James assured the Queen that 'there was no cause for alarm' – even though Albert was wandering from room to room talking gibberish. By the time a second opinion was called it was too late. The fever had taken a grip and Albert was a goner.

The Queen blames her husband for dying too easily. 'He would die,' she told Lord Derby, 'He seemed not to care to live.'

Today the whole nation is in mourning. The Prince will be sorely missed, most of all by his heartbroken wife.

Oddly enough, Albert had predicted his own death some years earlier.

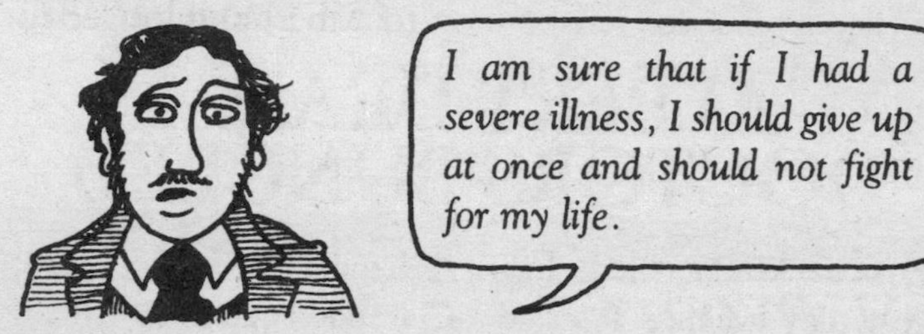

That's just how it turned out. Albert never clung on to life like Victoria. Whether he could have been saved by a decent doctor no one will ever know.

For Victoria it was as if the world had stopped turning. Without her dear Albert she felt that her life was over. This posed a bit of a problem since she was only 42 and, in fact, still had half her life in front of her. What would she do without her dear, wise Albert to lean on? The answer was: be miserable and make everyone else's life a misery too. A great gloomy black cloud was about to descend on Britain.

The great gloom

It was natural that Victoria should miss Albert. She'd loved him dearly and had come to depend on his advice in everything. However, Victoria wasn't planning on a year or two of mourning – she was planning on a lifetime! Not only that, she expected the whole country to mourn with her. It was time to paint the country black.

Albert was buried at Frogmore on the Windsor estate. A marble statue of the Prince was carved on top of his tomb. Victoria would visit often and spend hours there gazing on 'his beloved features' – although the features were only made out of stone. The Queen made sure she reserved a place for herself next to Albert and longed for the day when she could join him.

When she was younger, Victoria tried to be fashionable, from now on her only colour was black.

Victoria wore black for the rest of her days. Her ministers and servants also had to wear black and the nation followed their lead. Women wore black ostrich feathers in their hats, men wore black crepe 'weepers' (bands) round their top hats. Even the horses wore black plumes on their heads.

Six months after Albert's death, Victoria's daughter, Princess Alice, got married but the wedding was more like a funeral. All the guests were dressed in black and Victoria sat in her widow's weeds, frowning under a bust of Prince Albert. The wedding photographs must have been cheerful!

The dying trade

It's hard for us to understand the Victorian mania with death. Today dying is something we generally prefer not to talk about – although it's the one thing we can all count on. The Victorians were different. There was nothing they liked better than a good funeral. Maybe it's because death was much more common in the 19th century. If you were poor you were lucky to see your 40th birthday. Every day thousands of children died of hunger or disease. The Victorians accepted death as part of daily life, but that didn't mean they kept quiet about it. Grieving Victorian style was a public affair and the funeral trade was a huge industry.

The custom of wearing black dates from 1660, but it didn't catch on in a really big way until the Victorian age. There were actually shops in London that sold only black. Here's a typical advert from 1887.

It wasn't only clothes that were black, you could have your furniture dyed black as a mark of respect. Ribbons, fans and jewellery in black (called jet) were all available from shops dealing in the death trade. Naturally the shopkeepers assured their customers that they made no personal profit from their trade. The period of mourning varied according to the importance of the departed. When Queen Victoria's aunt – the Queen of Hanover – died in 1841, court mourning was a measly three weeks. Albert was another matter altogether. In 1869, eight years after his death, Victoria's servants were still wearing black armbands!

The hermit Queen

As for Victoria herself, her grief was so unbearable that she hid herself away. It would be 13 long years before she'd return to public life. Even then it would take all Disraeli's charm and cunning to draw her out of retirement.

What did the Queen do during those 13 long years? She stayed in Scotland and the Isle of Wight thinking of Albert. London was far too near Parliament and the horrid business of running the country. The only thing that would tempt Victoria out of hiding was the promise of someone putting up a memorial of her dear departed hubby. Victoria liked statues of Albert and she wanted lots of them. When Wolverhampton became the first town to erect a statue to Albert, Victoria turned up to unveil it. What's more, she knighted the Lord Mayor. If you fancied a knighthood, it was pretty clear what you had to do. Suddenly statues of Albert started to spring up all over the place!

If you take a short stroll from London's Hyde Park today, you'll walk through Albertopolis. There are lots of reminders of Victoria's Albert mania.

Albert lives

To Victoria, Albert wasn't dead, he was just a little more quiet than usual. When Lord Clarendon visited the Queen at Osborne House he had difficulty believing Albert wasn't in the room. Perhaps the visit got a mention in Victoria's journal.

VICTORIA'S SECRET DIARY

Lord C called to see me and I received him in my beloved's dear room. I have all dearest Albert's things set out on his table just as they used to be. His pen and blotting paper, his hanky on the sofa, his watch (still going) and fresh flowers. Spoke to Lord C at some length. We talked about Albert – I don't wish to hear about tiresome things like Acts of Parliament.

Every evening my dear one's clothes are laid out in his room for the morning. Every evening I have his chamber pot washed and cleaned. Over our bed hangs a photograph of him – on the right side where he always used to sleep. Never, ever ever shall I forget him! (And nor shall anybody else, I'll see to that.)

If Victoria was dead to the outside world, she wanted Albert's ghost to keep her company. Even when she went abroad she took Albert's photo with her to show him the view!

Royal sponger

After several years had passed, the public began to grow tired of the Queen's endless misery. Wasn't it time she got back to work? What was the point of a Queen who no one ever saw?

The newspapers and critics in Parliament started to grumble. Victoria's popularity took a nose dive and people begun to call her 'The Royal Malingerer' (lazybones). Some even whispered that she was off her head. Madness was in the family after all, it was said that George III used to talk to trees.

Mocking posters appeared outside Buckingham Palace:

There was one possible solution – Victoria would have to let her eldest son take over her public duties for her. But her eldest son, remember, was Bertie, Prince of Wales. Victoria had no intention of handing the reins over to *him*. When we last met Bertie he was pulling his teacher's beard. What had become of him in the meantime?

Bad Bertie – at it again

Bertie's strict education didn't end when he grew up. His parents were constantly bemoaning his stupidity and idleness. It never occurred to them that if they'd given him something to do he wouldn't have been so idle. Victoria was always moaning about her son's weakness and lack of brains.

To try and improve his brains and character, Bertie was packed off to university and then the army. At Oxford, Bertie was the most miserable student in the whole college. Not only was he forbidden to mix with other students of his own age, he was constantly under the eye of his aging minder, Major Robert Bruce. Bertie even had to write a note to ask for permission if he wanted to go out for a walk.

When he was almost 18, his parents still treated him like a naughty schoolboy. Victoria never visited him and Albert sent him notes – usually dreary lectures on education and duty.

It's hardly surprising that poor Bertie behaved badly. While he was in the army he started seeing a girlfriend.

But she wasn't a princess, she was an actress called Nellie Clifden. In those days the affair of the Prince and the actress caused a shocking scandal. It upset upright Albert no end (and he died soon after). Victoria said that she could never look at her eldest son without a shudder after that.

A marriage was quickly arranged to keep bad Bertie out of mischief. On 10 May 1863 Bertie was married to Alexandra, Princess of Denmark. (The Danish royal family were hard up and willing to overlook the Prince's fondness for actresses.)

Even Bertie's wedding day was ruined by his mum. Victoria, still mourning Albert, refused to attend the wedding service in St George's Chapel at Windsor. Instead, she watched it from a balcony room in her widow's dress – casting an air of gloom over the whole occasion.

She was hardly more cheery about the prospect of Bertie as the future king.

> *Oh! what will become of the poor country if I die!*
> *I foresee, if Bertie succeeds, nothing but misery. . .*
>
> REAL DIARY EXTRACT

A Highland fling

Of course, Victoria never dreamed that she could be capable of causing a scandal herself. Yet four years after Albert's death, tongues started to wag about the Queen and another man. Even more shocking, the man in question was one of the Queen's servants.

John Brown was a rough Scotsman who liked his whisky and spoke his mind.

Brown had been one of Albert's favourite servants at Balmoral so Victoria adopted him. Soon she couldn't do without him. Victoria's fondness for her Highland servant caused many a snigger. One rumour claimed that Brown was actually a medium who'd put Victoria in touch with Albert's ghost. Others gossiped that the Queen had actually married her rude Highlander in secret. People started to mockingly call Victoria 'Mrs Brown'.

In those days newspapers used to print polite court circulars informing readers what the royals were doing. Punch magazine printed an imaginary court circular as if Brown was royalty:

Court Circular

7th July 1866 Balmoral, Tuesday
Mr John Brown walked on the Slopes (of Windsor). He subsequently partook of a haggis. In the evening, Mr John Brown was pleased to listen to a bag-pipe.
Mr John Brown retired early.

Victoria didn't see the joke. Actually, since she never went out in public, she was ignorant of all gossip. The fact was, she didn't have any friends – they were all her subjects – and she wasn't close to her family. She needed a friend and chose Brown because he was blunt and honest. She even liked the way he sometimes scolded her like she was a little girl.

Brown tales

Here are a few of the stories about the Queen and her rude Scottish servant:

- Brown didn't call Victoria 'Your Majesty'; he called her 'wumman'.
- A passing tourist once heard him shouting at Victoria, after he'd pricked her chin trying to fasten her cape. 'Hoots, then, wumman!' he growled. 'Can ye no hold yerr head up?'
- Brown was fond of whisky and used to put a nip in the Queen's tea. On more than one occasion he was drunk as a skunk on duty. Victoria pretended not to notice.

VICTORIA'S SECRET DIARY

Waited for half an hour in my carriage this morning for Brown to come and take the reins. Fearing something must be wrong, I sent a footman to knock on his door. Brown appeared, but the poor man had to be supported all the way to the gate. He looked very unsteady on his feet and his breath smelt awfully! I can only think he must be exhausted from his many duties. How devoted he is!

When we arrived at the house, Brown tried to help me down. But, taking a step back, he swayed and fell flat on his face.

'Can he no' stand up?' asked our host, running out.

'I think there must have been a slight earthquake,' I told her.

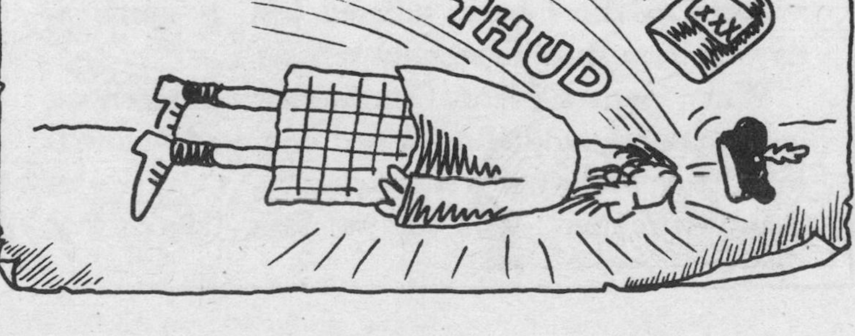

Victoria's children couldn't stand her Highland servant. Once Victoria's daughter, Vicky, was visiting, bringing the Queen's grandchild, little Princess Charlotte. The Queen commanded Charlotte to say hello to Brown.

Bertie was even less of a fan. After his mother died, he took personal pleasure in going round Windsor and smashing every bust of John Brown he could lay his hands on.

'HOW WE LAUGHED'
-Queen Victoria was amused

Visitors to the Queen suffered just as much as anyone from Brown's straight talking.

When General Henry Gardiner arrived he shook hands politely with Brown and enquired, 'How is the Queen and what is she saying?'

Brown replied, 'Well she just said, "Here's that

damned fellow Gardiner come and he'll be poking his nose into everything.'"

Brown once saved the Queen's life, when a man with a gun attacked her carriage at the gates of Buckingham Palace. Brown seized the young man by the throat and sat on him till the police arrived. He was given a gold 'Victoria Faithful Service Medal', an honour that was his and his alone.

Brown died in 1883, after 18 years' loyal service. He kept up his seven-days-a-week attendance on the Queen right to the end.

More than 20 years after his death, letters written by Queen Victoria about John Brown were discovered in a big black trunk. For some mysterious reason they were burnt. Could they have contained secrets that would have embarrassed the royal family?

One reason that Victoria doted on Brown was that he understood the things she couldn't abide – such as smoking. Bertie – a great cigar smoker – once adopted a room at Windsor as a secret smoking room for his pals. When he heard his mother was on the warpath, he escaped discovery by a clever dodge.

Smoking was just one of Victoria's pet hates. She had lots of others as the list below shows.

Queen Victoria's top ten pet-hates

1 Education for the workers.
'It is rendering the working class unfitted for good servants and labourers.'

2 Bishops.
'I do not like Bishops.'

3 Meeting people she knew when out for her afternoon drive.

4 Men staying behind after dinner while the ladies retired.
'I think it is a horrid custom.' Lord Melbourne was allowed a maximum of five minutes.

5 The hairstyle of the 1880s.
'The present fashion of fringe and frizzle in front is frightful.'

6 Cars.
'I am told that they smell exceedingly nasty, and are very shaky and disagreeable conveyances altogether.'

7 Votes for women.
'She ought to get a good whipping,' Victoria said of one suffragette.

8 Death duties.
She feared they would cause hardship to 'poor widows' (like herself).

9 Loud voices.

10 Getting her head wet when bathing in the sea.

Not that Victoria was perfect herself. She could be pig-headed and unforgiving. Another of the Queen's oddities was the way she spoke. Victoria had been brought up by a German mother and her grasp of English was never quite perfect. Her notes sometimes had a German flavour with odd spellings such as 'schocking' and 'bewhildering'. Sometimes she even got muddled up with her words.

When in Scotland, Victoria had a habit of copying the way her Highland servants spoke. She once asked a servant if he had any money to give one of the local cottagers. 'Aboot twelve shillings,' he replied.

'Ah that won't do a-tall, I always give her five poond,' said the Queen.

During the long years of mourning for Albert, Victoria wasn't so often amused. This is probably where her reputation as the Queen of Gloom started.

Yet it wasn't all bad news. While Victoria hid herself

away and moped, Britain continued to strengthen its position as the top dog in the world. It's time to look at some of the glories of the Great British Empire.

'WE ARE AN EMPRESS' - THE BRITISH EMPIRE

One hundred years ago Britain ruled the biggest empire the world has ever seen. At its biggest, one quarter of the world was under British rule. The Empire stretched from Canada to Australia and from India to South Africa. At its head was Victoria – the mother of this great family of nations. There was a famous saying at the time:

Since the Empire was so vast, the sun was always shining somewhere, either in London, Calcutta or Sydney. There was also another side to the boast. The British firmly believed that the sun would never go down on their glorious Empire. They were wrong – but it didn't start to crumble till after Victoria's time.

Maps of the world usually showed the British Empire in pink, blushing with modest pride. If you'd been a

Victorian schoolchild you'd probably have spent hours staring at maps like these.

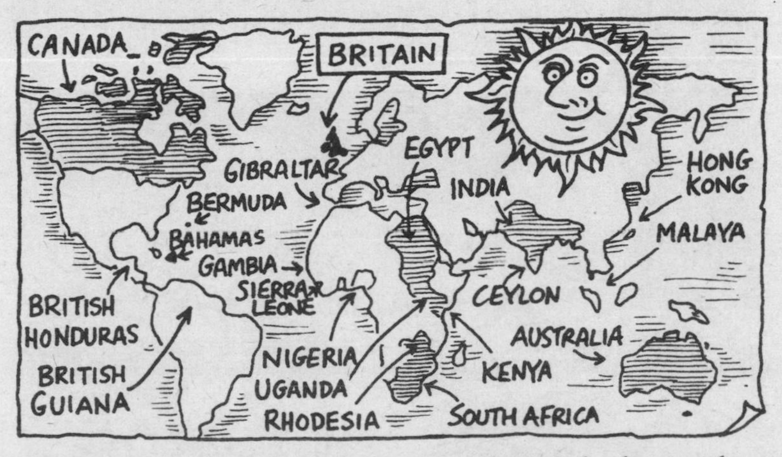

How did the British Empire get so big? It had started as far back as the reign of Good Queen Bess – Elizabeth I – when England began to establish new colonies. The Empire had grown slowly ever since. Not that Britain ever set out to conquer the world. The real prize was trade and wealth. By grabbing countries like India, Britain got rich from trading their goods.

During the 19th century the greedy European powers set about slicing the world into pieces like a giant cake. (Africa got carved up in 1884, though nobody bothered to tell the Africans.) Britain managed to grab the biggest slices of cake because it had the largest navy and controlled the trade routes at sea. Politicians behind this policy, such as Palmerston and Disraeli, were known as Empire builders. They piled their plates with cake and brought it to Victoria to be gobbled up into the British Empire. This attitude was known as Jingoism after a popular music hall song.

Not every country was keen to be ruled by the British which led to squabbles such as the Boer War and the Indian Mutiny. We'll come to these shortly. First, what had happened to Victoria after her years of playing hide and seek from her subjects?

The great comeback

By 1871, ten years after Albert's death, Victoria's popularity was at an all-time low. The gossip about 'Mrs Brown' was the talk of every London dinner party. In Parliament there were even MPs who talked openly about a Republic – government without royalty. No king or queen? It was enough to make the royal blood run cold! Even Victoria – who hadn't paid attention to anything for years – was alarmed.

By the following year, however, the Queen had made a triumphant comeback.

First, the nation was shocked when Bertie fell ill. For a time it looked as if he would follow his father to an early grave. At last, when he made a miraculous recovery the Queen attended a thanksgiving service at St Paul's Cathedral. She was back in business and the crowds cheered. All it needed was another assassination attempt for Victoria's popularity to be fully restored. As if on cue a pistol-waving maniac attacked her two days later and got flattened by big John Brown. (No one cared that the pistol wasn't loaded.)

The Queen's return to public life was helped by Disraeli – her pet Prime Minister. By 1876, the Queen had agreed to open Parliament again. In return for this service she made a small suggestion. For a long time, India had been part of the Empire so. . .

Victoria liked the sound of Empress of India, it had a nice ring to it. Disraeli, in return for this little gift, became the Earl of Beaconsfield. It was the crowning moment in an astonishing career for the Queen's favourite flatterer. For Victoria the crown of India was a bauble to be prized. All her life she had a great fascination for India, although she never visited it (far too hot). But her Indian subjects had a great respect for her. When she finally died, most of Calcutta's population sat in the park all day without food, mourning the great Queen-Empress that they'd never met.

Queen in disguise

Victoria never got to India but she did travel to other parts of the world. Sometimes she used to travel in disguise. It would be nice to record that she went round dressed as a policeman with a handlebar moustache, but Victoria's disguise was more subtle. It looked like this:

Yes, Victoria's cunning trick was to dress just like everybody else!

'I hate being troubled about dress,' she once said, so she only dressed like a queen when she had to. When off duty, it was hard to tell the Queen apart from her Ladies in Waiting or even from the servants. This sometimes led to embarrassing mistakes. A drunken gentleman called Dawson-Damer once went up to her and said:

When travelling abroad the Queen posed as the Countess of Kent. After all, you couldn't possibly expect her to pretend to be a commoner. Her daughter, Louise, would sign herself in the hotel register as the Lady Louise Kent.

Victoria delighted in going shopping in Paris in her 'ordinary person' disguise. In her elderly years she would make annual pleasure trips to Europe, especially to Nice in the sunny south of France. 'When one is in a country one likes to see some life about one,' said Victoria. She would drag her party endlessly through the countryside in search of a monastery or a soap-factory to visit.

Sometimes she travelled with other royalty. 'She was so kind and amiable and in good spirits,' recalled the Tsar of Russia, 'but from time to time she poked me in the eye with her parasol, which was less pleasant.'

'HOW WE LAUGHED' - Queen Victoria was amused

The Queen's travels didn't extend to the far-flung parts of her Empire. India and Africa were too hot for her and, in those days (before aeroplanes), too far away to travel to easily.

Still, she could always welcome her subjects to court. Most people think Victoria was very stiff and formal, but in fact she much preferred visitors from abroad to dress as normal. This almost caused a scandal when the natives of British Guiana arrived. Their normal dress was to be stark naked! However, the men were persuaded to wear a small loincloth to preserve the Queen's modesty. When the famous African chief Cetewayo came to court, Victoria was disappointed that 'he appeared in a hideous black frock and coat.'

Victoria much preferred the West African chief who she entertained at Windsor. At the end of his audience, Victoria asked him if he'd like anything as a souvenir of his visit. The Chief pointed to Victoria's widow's cap. 'Yes, mighty Queen: I should like to have a bonnet as Your Majesty is now wearing, and I should like to be the only chief entitled to wear it.'

The Queen was much amused by this request and gave instructions that one of her spare caps should be given to the Chief. Much later his photograph was sent to her.

Rotten war

Victoria took a deep interest in her Empire and followed the wars that sometimes threatened her colonies. She always found the prospect of war alarming. The invention of new guns and explosives meant that war in the 19th century was becoming, well . . . dangerous. British soldiers often got killed and injured. Victoria knew this because she visited her wounded soldiers in hospital and liked to present them with medals. One Christmas she even sent her soldiers thousands of boxes of chocolates. That's just one of the Empire Tales you can read below.

The Indian Mutiny, 1857

Odd Empire fact: The revolt in India was sparked by cow fat.

From the early 1800s much of India was controlled by the British East India Company. Their interest was trade rather than controlling India and its people. All this changed with the strange mutiny that broke out in parts of India in 1857. One cause of the revolt was a new rifle cartridge issued to Indian soldiers. (The British army in India had English officers but Indian soldiers.) A soldier had to bite off the end of the cartridge before pouring the powder into the barrel. Trouble started when a rumour went round that the cartridge was greased with fat. Worse still it was whispered the fat came from cows and pigs. This was an outrage to Hindus, who believe the cow is a sacred animal. Muslims were equally outraged because they regard pigs as 'unclean'.

Soon mutiny broke out all over northern India. At Delhi and Cawnpore many British were butchered. Queen Victoria was horrified.

What did Britain do? It sent 70,000 troops armed with the new American Colt revolver. The rebels were tortured and killed without mercy. Some of them were even tied to cannons and blasted. (But Victoria didn't mention these 'horrors'.)

The main result of the mutiny was that the East India Company's rule came to an end. A company that could allow cow fat to start a rebellion obviously wasn't fit to be in charge. From then on India came under the direct rule of the British crown.

The Crimean War, 1853–56

Odd Empire fact: The Crimean War was the first war where people at home read news reports from the front line and even saw war photographs.

The Crimean War is best remembered for two things: Florence Nightingale and the Charge of the Light Brigade. The Charge of the Light Brigade was made famous by Lord Tennyson's heroic poem:

There's pages more of it, but you get the general idea. Actually the Light Brigade's charge was one of the biggest blunders in British history – but since it was a heroic blunder nobody minded except the soldiers who got killed.

The Crimea wasn't even part of the British Empire. It was a peninsula that's now part of Turkey. The war was between the Turks and the Russians, but British troops were sent because of fears that Russia was getting too powerful.

The war was one in the eye for Victoria's great British Empire. British generals argued and bungled, soldiers died of disease, and troops were hopelessly short of supplies. Some found themselves with two left boots to wear in the freezing conditions.

Then came the Light Brigade's almighty clanger. Led by the Earl of Cardigan, they attacked the Russian guns in a cavalry charge down a long valley. It would have been a brilliant ploy, if they hadn't been charging in the wrong direction at the wrong enemy. They should have attacked the Russian flank. Instead, the 600 cavalry thundered down the valley towards the heavy artillery of Russia's main army. It was like attacking an angry bear with peashooters. Those who reached Russia's guns were left with no choice but to charge back the way they came while being shot at from all sides. Almost half of the Light Brigade died in the mad charge. A French general who saw it, General Bosquet, famously remarked: 'It's magnificent but it isn't war.'

A woman's place

Women weren't allowed to join the army in Victoria's day. A woman's role was to sit at home and be ladylike.

Times were changing, however, and some women weren't content to let men have all the action. One such woman was Florence Nightingale. When Florence heard that soldiers in the Crimea were dying without hospitals or doctors, she packed her lamp and went to help, taking 38 nurses with her. Before Florence, nursing was not considered a respectable profession for a woman (what with all that blood and sawing off of legs). Besides, the generals didn't want any women interfering in their army. They were making a hash of things quite well on their own. The wounded soldiers, however, regarded Florence as an angel and nicknamed her 'The Lady of the Lamp'.

A lamp wasn't the only thing she carried. As a pet lover, Florence often went round with an owl in her pocket. Back home in England she kept 60 cats, including two called Gladstone and Disraeli. Even the Queen was a fan and invited Florence to meet her.

In England, Florence set about improving the country's hospitals and made nursing a respectable profession for women.

Fetching bedpans was one thing but meddling in politics was another. The suffragette movement – which wanted votes for women – got no support at all from Victoria.

Funny that Victoria never had a problem telling her male Prime Ministers what to do.

The Boer War, 1899–1902

Odd Empire fact: During this war the Queen knitted woolly khaki scarves for her troops with her initials VRI on them.

The Boers were farmers who resented Britain adding South Africa to its Empire collection. For one thing it was their land, for another gold and diamonds had recently been discovered in the region. Britain sent a massive army to teach the upstart Boers a lesson but they fought back using guerrilla tactics.

That's 'guerrilla' tactics – fighting hit and run style. For a long time the Boers' makeshift troops succeeded in making the mighty British army look rather silly. One British general, Buller, was known as Sir Reverse because he retreated so often.

One of the war's strangest stories concerns a bugler in one of Buller's regiments, a 14-year-old boy called Arthur Dunn. During a battle the British were losing, young Arthur panicked and sounded the advance instead of the retreat. His company charged forward – straight into a river where many drowned and others were shot. Guess what happened to the bungling bugler?

Was he:

a) put in prison?
b) court-martialled?
c) declared a hero?

Answer: c) Arthur survived to become a war hero, mainly because the country was in desperate need of heroes. He was taken to meet Queen Victoria who presented him with a new silver bugle. Luckily she didn't ask him to play a tune.

Chocolate soldiers

Victoria herself took a keen interest in the Boer War. At Christmas 1899 she decided to send her loyal troops a present. What better than a box of the new treat called chocolate? Soon every soldier was shipped a chocolate bar with Victoria's head on the lid of the tin box. Almost 100,000 chocolate bars went to Africa but not all were eaten. Some soldiers were so proud of owning the Queen's chocolate that they took the tin back home unopened. Others claimed that the Queen's choccie had saved their lives. Private James Humphreys was one. He kept his tin in his soldiers' haversack. One lucky day, when he was shot in battle, the bullet went through the tin and lodged in the chocolate rather than Humphrey's back. The doctor treating the lucky soldier sent the life-saving choc box to Queen Victoria. A note suggested she 'would doubtless wish another box be sent to Private Humphrey'.

Eventually the British beat the Boers through sheer weight of numbers. Even after the worst disasters Victoria said:

One other consequence of the Boer War was the start of the Boy Scout movement. Its devil-may-care founder, Baden-Powell, deserves a space to himself...

The first Boy Scout

Did you know that before Baden-Powell rubbed two sticks together to start a fire, he was a famous spy and war hero?

During the Boer War, BP (as his soldiers called him) became a hero for defending a town called Mafeking. He held out for 217 days using home-made ammunition and guns made from drainpipes. Mafeking was finally relieved.

BP always had his own odd ways of doing things. Africans nicknamed him *Mhlalapanzi* – which means the man who lies down to shoot. Apparently BP once shot a hippo while lying on his back and firing between his legs. (Don't try this one at home!) Many of Baden-Powell's fellow officers thought he was a complete headcase. During the defence of Mafeking, BP printed stamps. It seemed an odd way to fight a war but Baden-Powell's stamps bore his own head instead of the Queen's. He claimed the idea was to keep up morale, but when Victoria heard, she didn't see the funny side.

When not working on his stamp collection, BP loved nothing better than to dress up in disguise and go off on a daring adventure. Once he was sent to find out about the guns in an enemy fortress. Instead of sneaking up under the cover of darkness, Baden-Powell disguised himself as a mad butterfly-collector. Armed with a butterfly net and a notebook he boldly walked around the fortress. His sketches of butterflies looked innocent enough but actually they contained cunningly hidden secret information. . .

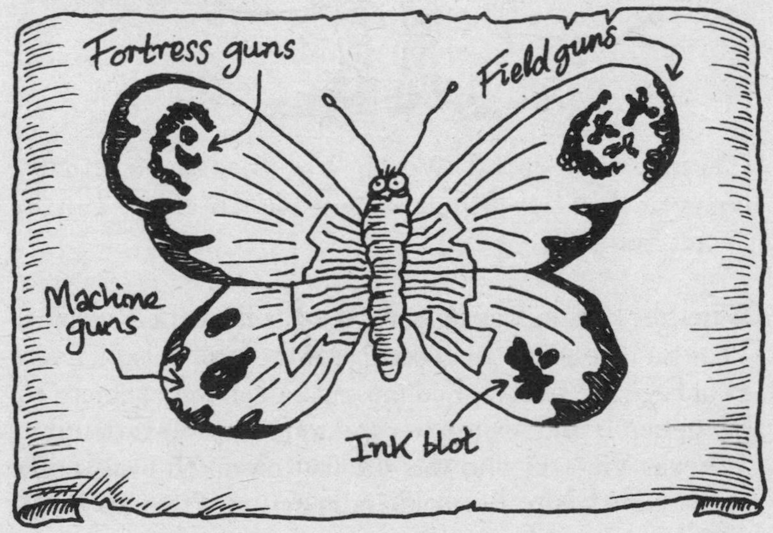

BP later wrote a thrilling book called *My Adventures as a Spy*. But it was his handbook for soldiers, *Aids for Scouting*, that gave him the idea for the Boy Scout movement. With a hero like Baden-Powell in charge, the idea of a boys' own club soon caught on. The first Scout uniform looked like this:

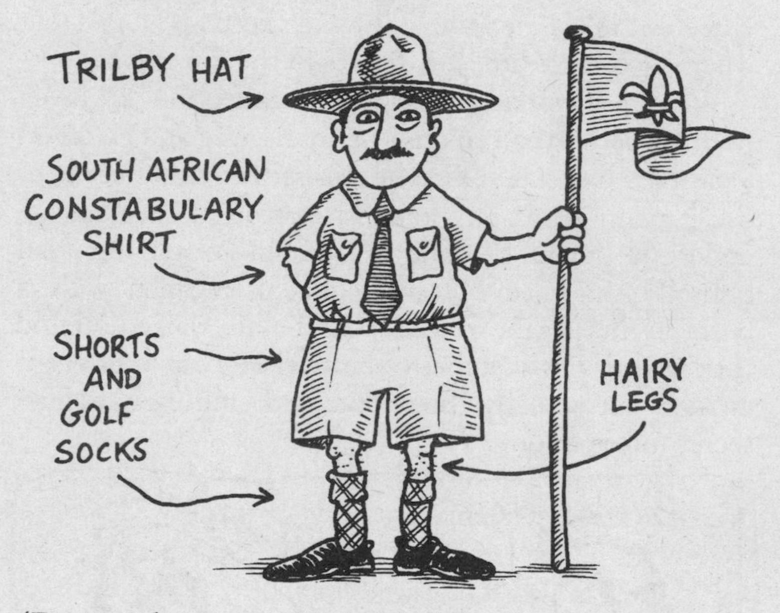

(During the Second World War the Nazis actually believed that Boy Scouts were a branch of the British Secret Service!)

Whether Britain was fighting the Boers or the Russians, Victoria embodied the fighting spirit of the nation. Even in old age she telegraphed messages of encouragement to her generals and visited her injured troops in hospital.

It was Victoria who was the first monarch to actually present medals to her soldiers *in person*. Previous kings had drawn the line at actually touching the hand of a common soldier, but Victoria thought nothing of taking such risks. She even invented a new medal for outstanding bravery – the Victoria Cross.

'HOW WE LAUGHED' ~Queen Victoria was amused

After the first time the Queen presented medals to her troops, Mrs Norton was talking to Lord Panmure about the unique event.

'Was the Queen touched?' she asked.

'Bless my soul, no!' was the reply. 'She had a brass railing before her, and no one could touch her.'

'I mean was she moved?' persisted Mrs Norton.

'Moved!' answered Lord Panmure, 'she had no occasion to move!'

Mrs Norton gave up.

Of course one day the sun would finally set on the glory of the British Empire. After the First World War its colonies eventually started to break away and Britain didn't have the resources to keep them. The Empire was gradually replaced by the Commonwealth – a kind of old boys' club for ex-members.

Victoria was probably glad she didn't live to see that day. The Queen was getting old and wobbly on her legs. One of her subjects wrote her a helpful letter suggesting that she ought to be attached to a hot-air balloon, so that she could float around rather than walk!

Yet even if she was doddery, Victoria's Britain was still Great Britain. Victorians were made of stern stuff and Baden-Powell wasn't the only one who became a hero. Whether it was writing novels, building ships or making scientific discoveries, the glorious Victorians led the world.

'We Are Proud' - Glorious Victorians

Victoria's reign lasted from almost the beginning of the 19th century to its end. It was a century of great change and invention. Take travel, for example. Victoria saw the first train rides and the first bicycles. She saw ships change from wood and sail to iron and steam. She even saw the first car (although she thought it would never catch on).

The Victorian age was the time when Britain really did think of itself as truly Great. Not only did Britain rule the biggest empire in the world, the British also liked to think they led the world in science, industry, art and literature. Names like Tennyson, Dickens, Brunel and Livingstone stood proudly for British achievement.

Life changed almost out of recognition during the Victorian age. At the beginning of her reign Victoria would have gone to bed by candlelight, but by the end she could read by the marvel of the electric light and even speak on the telephone.

VICTORIAN INVENTIONS
~ from the brilliant to the bonkers

Some inventions during Victoria's reign – such as the electric light and the telephone – changed the way that people lived. Other inventions – such as the Alarum Bedstead – have been completely forgotten, but they deserve a mention because they were so delightfully crackpot. Here's a brief selection of Victorian inventions, from the sensible and the sensational, to the nutty as a fruitcake.

1 The Alarum Bedstead

Oversleeping? Finding it hard to get out of bed in the morning? Dozy Victorians could always try the ingenious Alarum Bedstead. Not only would it wake you up but it made sure you got out of bed as well!

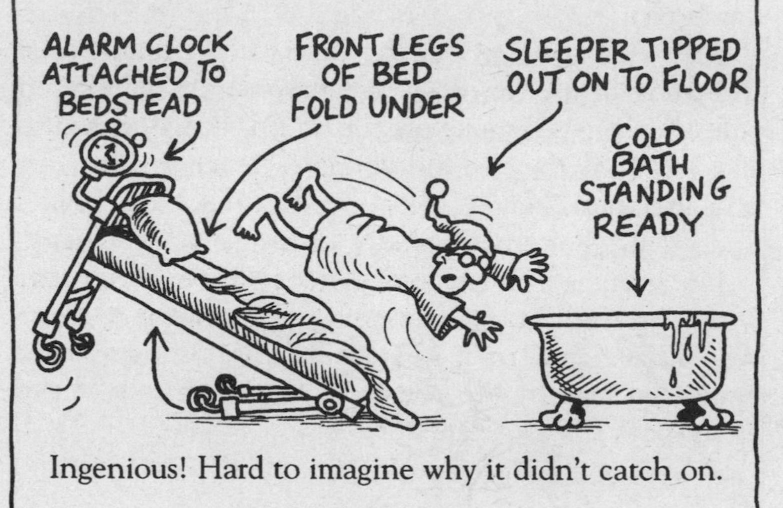

Ingenious! Hard to imagine why it didn't catch on.

2 The post box

Before 1840 ordinary people couldn't post letters as there was no postal service. The first post boxes were installed on the island of Jersey in 1852 – the brainwave of the Victorian novelist Anthony Trollope. Post boxes soon followed in London, and the first ones were hexagonal (six-sided) rather than round like modern pillar boxes. In London you can go spotting Victorian post boxes ...

3 The Sociable bicycle

The early days of bicycles saw inventors pedalling some truly batty ideas. One was the Sociable (1882) which tried to make riding a bike more . . . well, sociable. Two riders sat side-by-side between two enormous wheels, steering with a smaller wheel out in front. The idea was that you could chat to each other as you went along. This could lead to nasty accidents which perhaps explains why the Sociable wasn't a wheel success.

4 The telephone

The telephone was invented by a Scot, Alexander Graham Bell. He visited Queen Victoria at Osborne House on 14 January 1878 to demonstrate his startling invention. Victoria's verdict?

5 The shower

The first shower appeared in the mid 1800s, though it wasn't much like the power-showers we know today. The Victorian version was a tall curtained tent with a lid punctured with holes on top. A line of servants had to pass jugs of water to a maid on a ladder who poured the water into the lid and down onto the bather. Not surprisingly only the rich could afford to take a shower.

6 The speaking tube

Another invention that appeared in the Victorian home around 1850. Many servants lived in their own quarters and it was a tiresome nuisance for the master or mistress to have to shout downstairs for them. With the handy new invention you could simply whistle down the tube to call for attention.

7 Loos and rolls

Toilets and their unsavoury stinks were a problem even for royals like Prince Albert. The first public loo opened in 1852. It closed soon after as the public objected to paying two pence to spend a penny. (It cost another two pence to wash your hands.) Toilets for the home came in all kinds of designs and with marvellous names like Niagara Falls, Waterloo, Deluge and Crapper. The invention of perforated toilet paper was the brainwave of Walter James Alcock in the 1880s. However, tear-off loo paper wasn't easy to market to the prudish Victorians.

8 Strike a light
Before the 1820s, getting a spark to light a fire or a pipe was a slow business involving a tinder-box. Then English chemist John Walker was struck with a sure-fire idea: a light on a stick! The first matches were nicknamed Lucifers and were soon followed by the inventions of phosphorous and safety matches.

9 Chocolate bars
Chocolate had mouths watering at the Great Exhibition of 1851. Two years earlier Fry's of Bristol unwrapped what they claimed was the world's first moulded choc bar. Jelly Babies followed in 1864 and by the end of the century the Victorians were sucking up to Liquorice Allsorts.

10 The steam aeroplane
'Victorians have the steam ship and the steam train, so why not the steam plane?' That was the question asked by Scottish inventor, Joseph Kaufmann. Kaufmann designed a plane powered by a steam engine with wings that flapped up and down. He boasted it could travel through the air at 50 miles an hour (80 kph). Unfortunately, when he built a small model in 1869 the wings flapped so violently that the whole plane fell to bits.

'HOW WE LAUGHED' -Queen Victoria was amused

When they weren't inventing daft machines, Victorians liked to be royally entertained. There was a wealth of talent to choose from. The poorer classes went to the music hall which offered entertainment ranging from acrobats and jugglers to popular songs.

In 1844 the great American showman Phineas T. Barnum brought his company to London. Victoria's tastes were as lowbrow as any of her subjects and she was eager to see 'General' Tom Thumb, the pocket-sized entertainer – only 37 inches (97 cms) high. Barnum and the General were summoned to appear at Buckingham Palace. After running through his repertoire of songs, dances and impressions, the General was attacked by Victoria's poodle as he tried to make his exit walking backwards. (It was rude to turn your back on the Queen.)

The richer classes could choose from theatre, concerts or opera. The Queen could choose from anything she liked. Going to the theatre was such a drag so Victoria often had the theatre brought to her. An entire stage play and its cast would be transported to Windsor or Balmoral. This was expensive but Victoria didn't need to worry about that. Entertainments ranged from the Royal Opera to Welsh male voice choirs and performances of Shakespeare or Victorian melodramas.

The Queen also loved amateur theatricals and thought nothing of dragging all her children, servants and secretaries into a private performance. If anything in the play offended her she simply had it cut or changed. For example, a performance of the play *She Stoops to Conquer* led to problems when royals mixed with commoners – usually members of the Queen's household.

The Queen came to the rehearsals, which frightened us all very much. When she saw me chucking [stroking] Princess Louise under the chin (I was supposed to mistake her for a barmaid) she thought this was overdone. I received a message that I had better not indulge in any chucking under the chin.

Fritz Ponsonby – son of Victoria's Private Secretary.

We are not amused

How did Victoria's famous catch phrase come about? There are several versions of the story. One tale involves an unfortunate subject who dared to do an impression of Queen Victoria to her face. The unfortunate Admiral Maxse – at the Queen's request – was said to have put a hanky on his head and blown out his cheeks.

Victoria told him: 'We are not amused,' in her iciest voice.

That tale sounds far-fetched. Another, likelier, version involves Victoria's master of entertainment, Sir Alick Yorke. During a dinner party at Windsor, Sir Alick told a rude joke to a German visitor who made the mistake of laughing too loudly. The Queen immediately demanded that Yorke tell her what had caused so much amusement. Yorke repeated the story and got the famous reply. (You may remember Victoria is supposed to have used the words to Gladstone too!)

It's a pity that the famous phrase has made people think of Victoria as a grumpy old trout who couldn't take a joke. She was often amused with a laugh that could be heard halfway down the street.

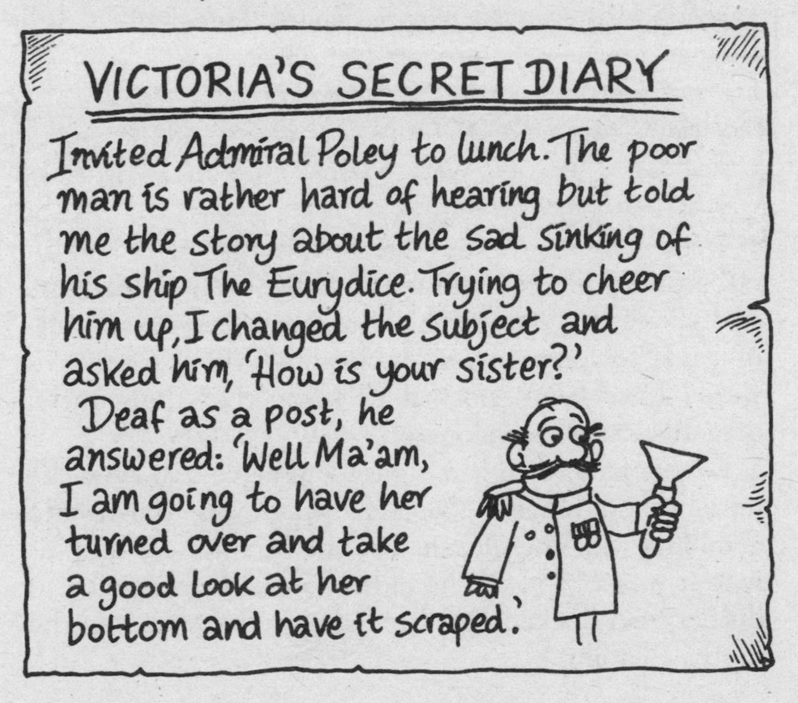

> You can't imagine how much I laughed! I had to put down my knife and fork and hide my face in my handkerchief. I shook till the tears rolled down my face. Meanwhile the poor Admiral was quite ignorant of what he'd said.

Game for a laugh

Victoria also enjoyed playing games. Her diary during the period when she proposed to Albert says:

> *I played two games of Tactics with dearest Albert, and two of Fox and Geese. Stayed up till 11.20 p.m., a delightful evening.'*

Albert would have preferred to invite men of literature and science to court but his wife much preferred a game of cards to long-winded discussions. Many Victorians would have been shocked to know that their queen actually *gambled* for money.

One popular card game was Commerce and even the upright and religious Mr Gladstone was drawn into gambling with the Queen. On one occasion he told his wife it was a good job he didn't lose as before going to dinner he'd 'locked up his purse'. (Perhaps to stop the moths escaping.)

Victoria's pleasures were simple and she was easily amused. While Shakespeare and the opera were considered to be 'respectable' theatre, Victoria preferred silly comedies and melodramas and laughed louder than anyone. At court she entered into any game such as charades or guessing riddles with great enthusiasm.

Glorious Victorians

Great Britain wouldn't have been half so great without some of the big names of the day. Victoria was a great lover of novels and poetry and was a big fan of Charles Dickens and Lord Tennyson, to name just two. With so many glorious Victorians to choose from it's hard to say who was the greatest or most influential. Perhaps we should ask Victoria herself?

CHARLES DICKENS

Claim to fame: Telling a good story. Dickens penned whopping big novels like *David Copperfield* and *Oliver Twist* (the musical came much later).

He'd got to pick a pocket or two? Despite growing rich, he never stopped worrying about being poor. He made extra money with public readings which were as popular as train rides, though not as smutty.

Victoria's view: The Queen was Charlie's number one fan. She once gave him a copy of her own book and signed it, 'from the humblest of writers to one of the greatest.'

What the Dickens? Dickens was terribly smitten with the Queen before her wedding. He confessed, 'I am sorry to say I have fallen hopelessly in love with the Queen, and wander up and down with vague and dismal thoughts of running away with a Maid of Honour.'

THE BRONTË SISTERS

The Spice Girls of their day? Be serious. Anne, Charlotte and Emily were novelists at a time when women were meant to stick to pressing flowers. Charlotte's book, *Jane Eyre*, is a classic romance. Emily's *Wuthering Heights* is a dark tale of passion and betrayal.

Not many giggles then? What do you expect? The Brontës were raised in a gloomy vicarage on the Yorkshire Moors.

Because women weren't supposed to write novels, they even had to write under false names to get their books published.

Victoria's view: The Queen read *Jane Eyre* and thought it, 'awfully thrilling.'

OSCAR WILDE

Claim to fame: Writing clever theatrical comedies such as *The Importance of Being Earnest*.

Tell us a joke, Oscar! Wilde was a great wit and had Victorian audiences rolling in the aisles. His specialty was turning ideas upside down. Example: 'There is only one thing worse in the world than being talked about, and that is not being talked about.'

Was he talked about? A lot. Especially when it became known he was gay (which was illegal then). It shocked Victorian society and Oscar was sent to jail. His health never recovered and he died in exile. Legend says that his last words were: 'Either that wallpaper goes or I do.'

Victoria's view: Not recorded. Oscar said the Queen was one of the three women he admired most and would have married with pleasure. (The other two were an actress and a singer.)

ISAMBARD KINGDOM BRUNEL

Is he what? A big name for a little man with a huge reputation. Brunel was an engineer who stood 5' 4" tall in his socks. He puffed on big cigars and wore a stove-pipe top hat into which he stuffed his papers when going on a journey. Two of his big ideas were the Clifton Suspension Bridge (still standing in Bristol) and the *Great Western*.

Great Western? Was he a cowboy builder? Ha ha! Actually, the *Great Western* was a monster ship – the fastest steamer to cross the Atlantic in its day.

Worst move: Isambard went on to build an even bigger ship – the *Great Eastern*. In fact it was so big it got stuck in the dock and took two months to launch. By then Brunel was bankrupt.

Victoria's view: The Queen wasn't on speaking terms with builders. Especially if they smoked cigars.

ARTHUR, LORD TENNYSON

Claim to fame: Victorian poet.

Give us a rhyme, Arthur! Tennyson's most famous poem was *In Memoriam*. Since it was sad and about death and mourning, it was right up the Queen's street. Tennyson wrote a poem for Victoria too, proving he could creep with the best of them. Example:

Her court was pure, her life serene
God gave her peace, her land reposed;
A thousand claims to reverence closed
In her as Mother, Wife and Queen.

Victoria's view: The Queen's fave poet and a lifelong chum. Victoria liked his bluntness. Once at Osborne,

Tennyson grumbled that he was always being pestered by intruders at his house. Victoria said she herself wasn't much troubled by them. To which Tennyson replied, 'Perhaps I shouldn't be either if I could stick a sentry at my gates.'

DAVID LIVINGSTONE

Claim to fame: Great Scot! – A Highland missionary and explorer.

Up Loch Ness with a paddle? Africa was more Livingstone's line. He discovered the Victoria Falls on his 4,000-mile trek across Africa. In 1866 he went back to find the source of the Nile, but vanished for several years. American Henry Stanley went to try and locate him.

Don't tell me – Stanley got lost too? No, he found him. Their meeting is famous. Stanley doffed his hat and said 'Dr Livingstone I presume?' Livingstone raised his cap and smiled, 'Yes.' (Great Victorians were awfully polite even at historic moments.)

Victoria's view: Livingstone died in 1873 – the only missionary to be honoured with a national funeral in Westminster Abbey. Victoria didn't go but she sent a nice wreath.

CHARLES DARWIN

Claim to fame: Biologist who invented the theory of evolution in his blockbusting book *The Origin of Species*.

Anybody read it? In a nutshell Darwin claimed that all life had 'evolved' from the same ancestors. Famously this made monkeys out of our early relatives.

Give the man a banana! Many Victorians wanted to give him a punch on the nose. Darwin's theory caused a mighty stink since it challenged the Bible's version of Creation (there's no mention of monkeys). Darwin was accused of blasphemy and the public outcry made him ill.

Victoria's view: The Queen was often surrounded by hairy apes but they were the government.

So if you had to choose, who was the most Glorious Victorian of them all?

No contest.

'WE ARE OLD' - THE JUBILEE YEARS

Queen Victoria was getting on a bit. As her Golden Jubilee approached – a half century on the throne – she was heading towards her seventies. By the end of the century she would have reigned longer than any king or queen in British history.

She was more tired than she used to be and still missing dear Albert, but she wasn't ready to quit. If there was one thing Victoria believed in it was doing her duty, and it was her duty to carry on as queen until her dying breath. In her sunset years Queen Victoria became the fat little old lady dressed in black that we know from photographs. Even for her big Jubilee party she would refuse to put on her crown and dress like a queen.

Little Big Queen

The Queen wasn't getting any thinner. By her 50s she had already reached a porky 12 stone. At about five feet tall she looked like a little black battleship. In old age she went on eating and getting fatter. The first diet was published in 1867 but Victoria for one didn't bother to read it. Her doctor, Sir James Reid, recommended a milky cereal called Benger's food. Victoria liked it but simply added it to the rest of her daily menu.

She needed a walking stick to get around and her eyesight wasn't so good, but there was nothing wrong with her appetite. Victoria liked rich foods like brown Windsor soup laced with a drop of wine. Boiled chicken, potatoes and peas were also favourites, as was mutton. When staying at Balmoral she was fond of haggis – a tempting Scottish delicacy made of offal (hearts, livers, lungs and other yummy stuff) wrapped in the stomach of a cow or sheep.

The Queen was fond of pastries and puddings too – strawberries and cream, if on offer, but she would just as happily tuck into a home-made toffee cake.

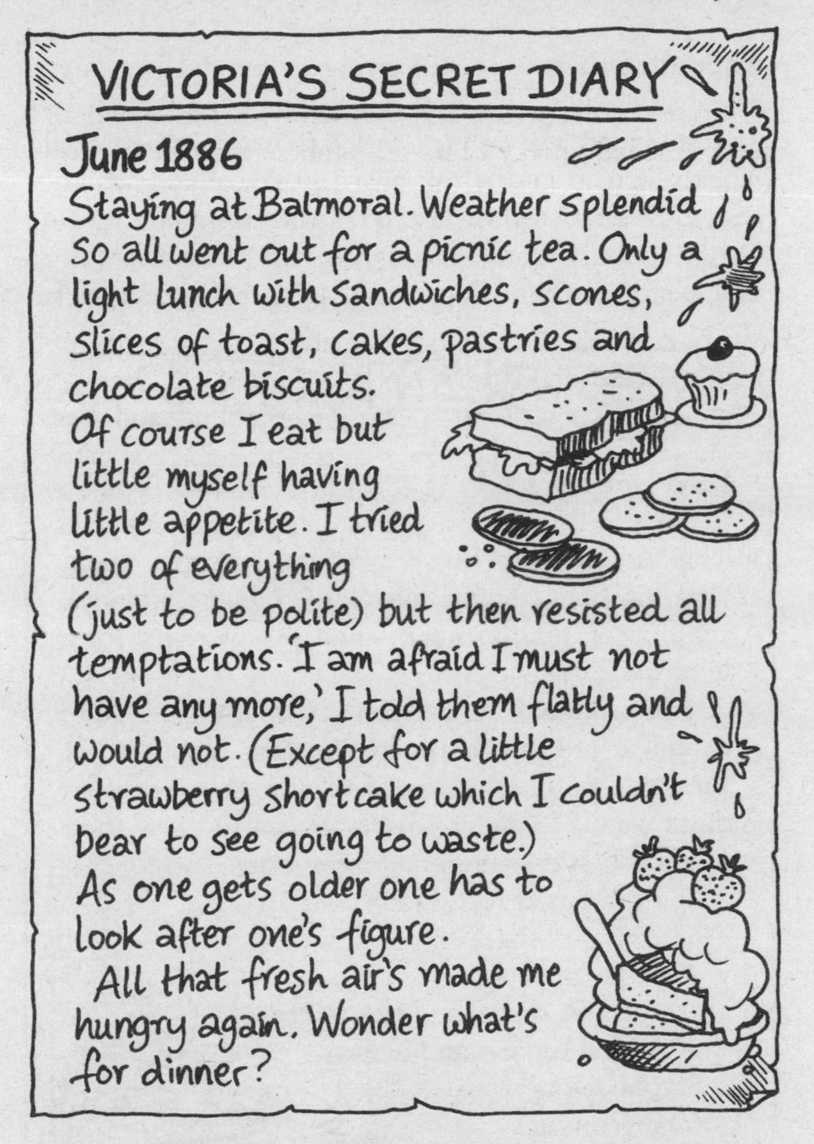

Victoria was a fast eater which gave her the advantage over her dinner guests. If there was a choice of either hot or ice puddings on the menu, she'd help herself to both, while the others were still trying to decide! Her guests often suffered as a result of her speed eating. When Her Majesty's plate was empty, scarlet-coated footmen would quickly appear and whisk away all the plates whether people had finished or not. This was too much for one visitor, hungry Lord Hartington, who saw his dinner disappearing out the door and roared, 'Bring that back!'

Food glorious food

If the Queen made a pig of herself, her subjects were just as porky. In a rich house the cooks might serve up ham, tongue, pheasant, kippers, kidneys, eggs, bacon and porridge – and that was just for a light breakfast!

The Guildhall in London saw many great state banquets but probably the greatest one was for Victoria's coronation in 1837. On that occasion there were 570 guests who managed to chew their way through enough food for an army:

200 tureens of turtle soup
45 dishes of shellfish
2 barons of beef
10 sirloins, rumps and ribs of beef
50 boiled turkeys and oysters
80 pheasants
60 pigeon pies
45 hams

140 jellies
200 ice creams
40 dishes of tarts
100 pineapples and more

There were 39 dishes in all. It's no wonder Victorian magazines were always advertising pills for heartburn and wind!

Poor people, on the other hand, didn't get much of a chance to eat ice cream. In the workhouse the daily menu was a revolting porridge called gruel. It was made from ground oatmeal and served as thinly as possible.

Those workers who had a roof over their heads often lacked a stove to cook their food. If you could afford some meat it could be taken to the bake-house where it would be cooked for a small fee. Market stalls in Victorian streets often sold hot chestnuts, potatoes or tea because the poor couldn't get hot meals at home.

Party plans

As the 50th birthday of her reign approached, Victoria was as popular as she'd ever been. The years of hiding after Albert's death were forgotten and Victorians were queuing up to sing the praises of their Queen. Fifty years on the throne was not to be sniffed at, especially for those who remembered the bad old days of the monarchy before Victoria.

Plans for the great Jubilee party were soon drawn up. The Viceroy of India wrote that 'all the ladies of Calcutta are ordering Jubilee bustles.' Over one million 'Women of England' signed a petition urging the Queen to close pubs on a Sunday. Victoria, who preferred whiskey in her tea to milk, turned a deaf ear.

A collection was taken up for the Jubilee, raising £75,000 in Britain alone. What was to be done with it? Should the money go to the poor, to hospitals, to the unemployed? Victoria was in no doubt.

There were rumours that Victoria might use the Jubilee to stand aside in favour of her son, Bertie. Anyone who believed that didn't know Victoria. She told her friends, who passed it on to Bertie, that he was unfit to be king and that she hoped to outlive him. Poor Bertie was always the black sheep of the family though he tried his best to please his mum. His New Year present to her was a Jubilee inkstand. When you opened the lid you saw the Queen's head and her face reflected in a pool of blue ink. 'Very pretty and useful,' remarked Victoria. Soon Jubilee souvenirs were selling like hot cakes. Here are a few useful items you could have bought in London.

The real party got underway on 20th June. By then the whole of the country was bubbling with excitement. The celebrations began with a modest family lunch – 50 kings, queens and princes from all over Europe. All of them were Victoria's relatives. She sat wedged between the Kings of Denmark and Greece while the Belgian king sat opposite her. The light lunch didn't cater for vegetarians – it included cold beef, roast fowl, venison steaks, chicken, veal and roast lamb – all served on dishes of gold plate. The next day came the procession to Westminster for a service of thanksgiving.

THE HARD TIMES

21st June 1887

GOD BLESS HER!

When the great day came, Queen Victoria did it her own way, as she has done for the last 50 years. No glass coach, no robes of state, no crowns and sceptres. Just a small figure dressed in a black dress and bonnet surrounded by no less than 32 princes of Europe.

'There she was a little old lady coming to church to thank God for the long years in which she had ruled her people,' said one eyewitness.

It's said the Queen wept at the start of the day – perhaps overcome with the occasion. Crowds thronged the streets on the way to Westminster Abbey and the cheering and applause was thunderous. After the service the royals filed past the Queen. Typically she stepped forward and embraced each of them in turn. What dignity! What majesty! What a pity about that hat!

Victoria wrote in her journal...

This never to be forgotten day will always leave the most gratifying and heart stirring memories behind.

REAL DIARY EXTRACT

That was the official story anyway. In fact the little old lady was 'half dead with fatigue' by the end of the day. And the next day the celebrations started all over again! Maybe Victoria's real feelings were less 'gratifying' than she pretended.

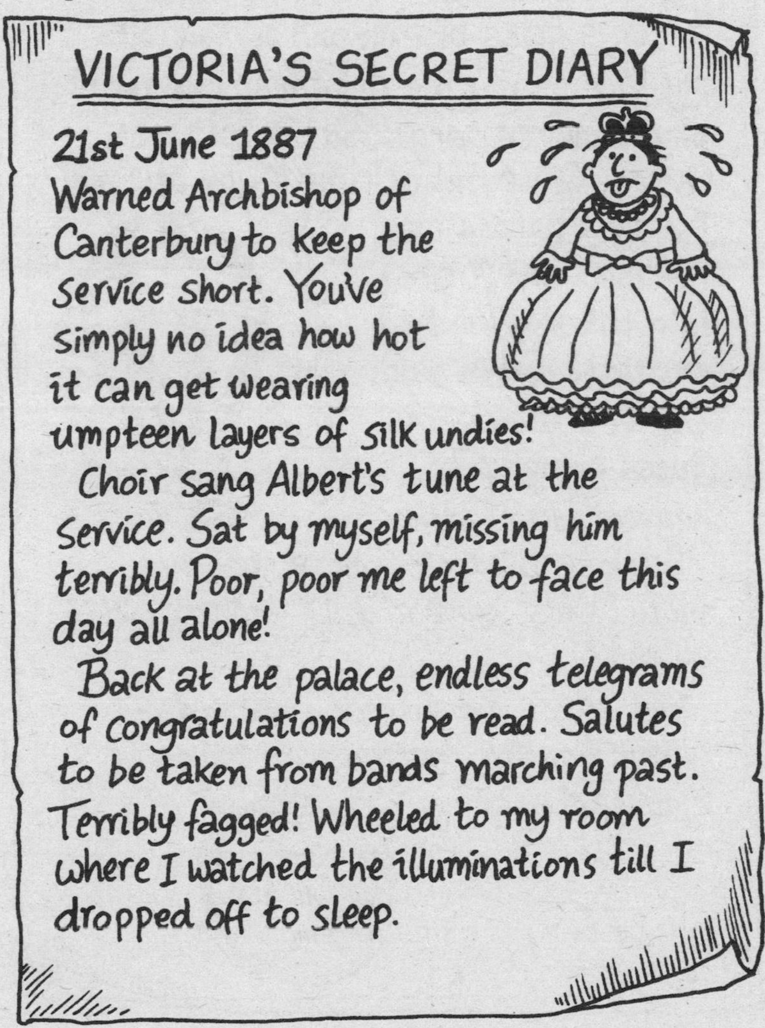

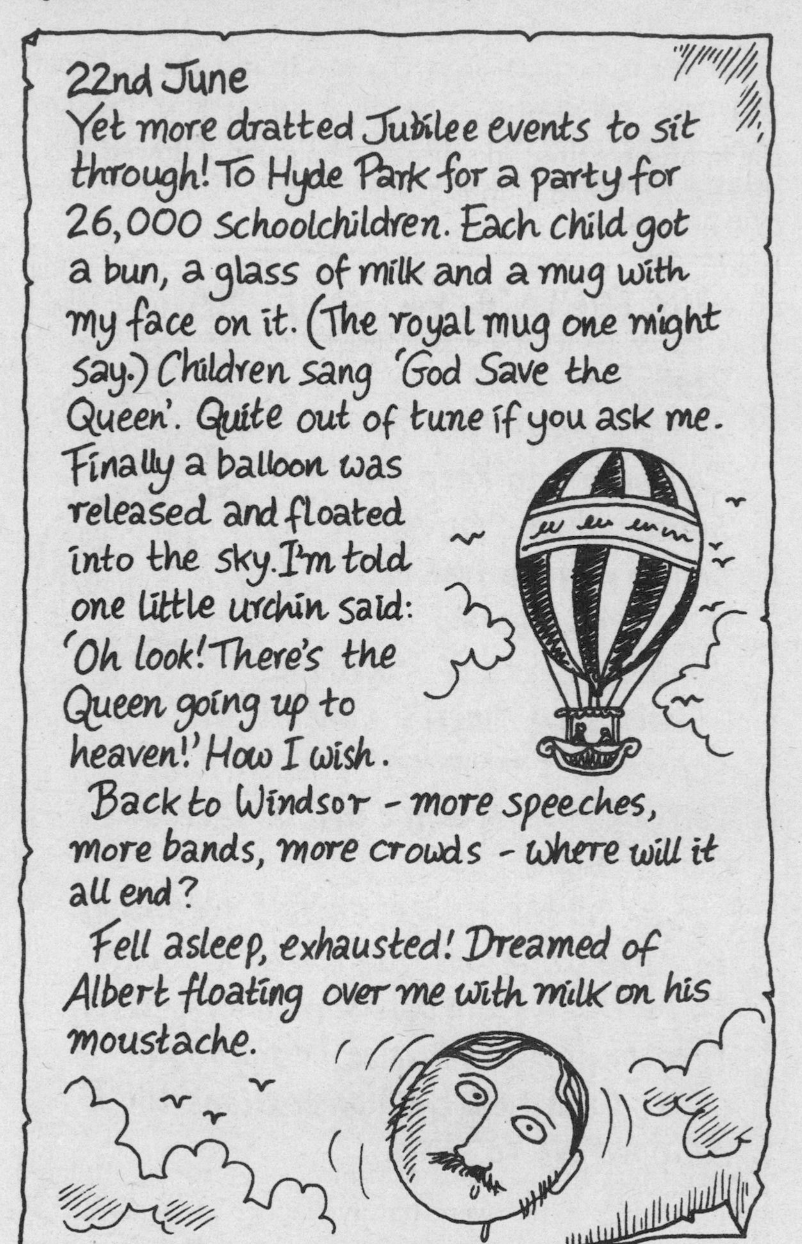

22nd June

Yet more dratted Jubilee events to sit through! To Hyde Park for a party for 26,000 schoolchildren. Each child got a bun, a glass of milk and a mug with my face on it. (The royal mug one might say.) Children sang 'God Save the Queen'. Quite out of tune if you ask me. Finally a balloon was released and floated into the sky. I'm told one little urchin said: 'Oh look! There's the Queen going up to heaven!' How I wish.

Back to Windsor - more speeches, more bands, more crowds - where will it all end?

Fell asleep, exhausted! Dreamed of Albert floating over me with milk on his moustache.

Only one thing went wrong during the celebrations, but Victoria never mentioned it in her official diary. During the impressive fireworks display a bouquet of flowers was supposed to change into a huge blazing portrait of the Queen's head. Unfortunately some faulty fireworks meant that the right eye of the Queen blinked on and off. It looked just as if she was winking at the crowds. We don't know if Victoria was amused.

Idle servants – Munshi-mania

Victoria did give herself one Jubilee present during the year. She'd often wished she could visit India, but since the country was far too hot, she brought a bit of India to England. The Empress sent for two Indian servants who promptly knelt and kissed her feet on their arrival. However the younger one, Abdul Karim, was by no means a crawler. Karim claimed to be the son of an Indian doctor (actually a prison chemist). He soon made it clear he was not a common servant.

Karim was known as the *Munshi* – Victoria's Indian secretary. His duties were hardly taxing. He waited on the Queen to dry the ink of her signature and gave her lessons in Hindustani. The Munshi proved himself a splendid successor to John Brown and he was just as unpopular at court as the rude Scotsman.

Black-bearded and turbanned, the Munshi gave himself airs above all the other servants. Once, when asked to sit with the servants to watch a play, he refused and went to sulk in his room. After that he generally ate with the Queen's own household, including the Lords and Ladies in Waiting who hated the sight of him.

The Munshi was given a furnished house at Osborne where large numbers of his relatives claiming to be his wife and aunts came and went. Dr Reid, the Queen's doctor, remarked that every time a Mrs Karim fell ill, a different tongue was put out for him to examine.

The general contempt for the Munshi was partly Victorian prejudice, but it's true he lorded it over even his fellow Indian servants. Matters came to a head when the Queen's household finally rebelled. On a trip to France they told the Queen that it was the Munshi or them – she'd better choose. Victoria went into a rage and swept all the papers off her desk. Finally it was decided the Munshi would not travel in the Queen's train but follow in an ordinary one. But the more people complained about the Munshi, the more Victoria defended him.

Ladies in Waiting

Queen Victoria was surrounded by vast numbers of staff. On a holiday trip to France, she declared she couldn't manage without less than a hundred. Not all of them were servants, some of them were the Queen's companions. What exactly did a Lady in Waiting do (besides waiting around)? Their duties included looking nice on state occasions and gossiping with the Queen. If there were visitors the Queen's Ladies looked after them and they also had to scribble down the endless notes that Victoria was in the habit of sending.

The Queen's Lords and Ladies were carefully selected...

When Marie Adeane was first approached to become a Maid of Honour (a sort of junior Lady in Waiting) she was presented with a four-part questionnaire.

QUESTIONNAIRE

1. Does the candidate read and write French and German? . . . .
2. Can she play the piano, so as to play duets with the Princess Beatrice? . . . .
3. Horseback riding: what proficiency can she show? . . . . .
4. Is she engaged to be married or likely to be? . . . . . .

Victoria didn't like members of her household getting married. It was so inconvenient for her to lose her staff. 'It is too tiresome,' she said when her doctor, Sir James Reid, married one of her young Maids of Honour.

It must have been a dull life at times: breakfast at 9.30, luncheon at 2 p.m., a drive in the afternoon, dinner at 9 p.m. and a little music in the drawing room before Her Majesty's yawn signalled it was time for bed. At least there were occasional funny moments. Once, a nervous Maid of Honour sang for the Queen but forgot to remember the tremolos (wobbly notes to you). 'Does she not shake?' asked the Queen. 'Oh yes, ma'am,' replied the girl's mother, 'she's shaking all over.'

'HOW WE LAUGHED' -Queen Victoria was amused

Victoria's sense of humour was once tickled at Balmoral by a bustle (a sausage-shaped object used to pad dresses). Just as the Queen was going out of the room she stepped on something which turned out to be somebody's bustle. All the ladies present promptly denied it was theirs. Lord Knutsford said it looked like Sir Henry Ponsonby's, which reduced Victoria to fits of giggles. Eventually the head butler solemnly announced that the 'property' belonged to the Duchess of Roxburghe. A page presented the large sausage to the red-faced Duchess who denied ever having seen it. The Queen was by this point helpless with laughter. Finally the mystery was solved when one of the maids owned up to having lost her bustle.

Bad Bertie – all grown up and nothing to do

'Gangan', as Victoria's grandchildren called her, was entering her 70s. Meanwhile her middle-aged son, bad Bertie, was still waiting in the wings. As far as Victoria was concerned he could wait for ever. She never believed he would make a good king. The model of manhood, in Victoria's view, was dear dead Albert, and Bertie was as different from his father as beer from champagne.

By the 1890s Bertie was an ageing, plump playboy with nothing better to do than bet on racehorses and chase women. (Bertie had married Princess Alexandra in 1863, but this didn't stop him having other 'girlfriends'.) Victoria disapproved of his 'fast' way of life, moving from one party or racecourse to the next.

But Bertie didn't want to be solid and dutiful. He liked parties and practical jokes with his rich pals. One of his cronies, Christopher Sykes, was sometimes made to crawl around under the table saying 'As your Royal Highness pleases,' while Bertie splashed brandy down his neck. When he was king, one of Bertie's favourite pranks was to leave a dead bird or a dried pea in one of his guest's beds. Victoria would certainly not have been amused.

Victoria hated the thought of Bertie becoming king. But she had to face facts – she couldn't go on for ever. One thing she'd always enjoyed was a good funeral and she knew it wouldn't be long before her own.

'WE ARE DEPARTED' - THE END AT LAST

Queen Victoria still had one last hooray left. On 22nd June 1897 she celebrated her Diamond Jubilee. It was a record-breaking occasion. She'd spent 60 years on the throne. That meant she'd reigned longer than any other British monarch in history.

Unlike the Golden Jubilee party which was a family affair, the Diamond Jubilee was a celebration of the glorious British Empire.

THE HARD TIMES

22nd June 1897

EVERY INCH A QUEEN

They came from every corner of the Empire to wish her well. Canadian Mounties, Jamaican artillery, giant Maories, troops from New Zealand, China, South Africa, and the magnificent bearded lancers of the Indian Empire. The procession stretched as far as the eye could see.

At the back was a carriage drawn by eight cream-coloured horses. Through a storm of waving hankies, past thousands of eager faces, and wave upon wave of cheers came Queen Victoria. 'So very quiet, so very grave, so very punctual, so unmistakably and every inch a Queen,' as one eyewitness put it.

The service at St Paul's was kept short out of respect for the Queen's age and poor health. Afterwards even the Archbishop of Canterbury got carried away with the occasion and called for three cheers for the Queen. The echo could have been heard by Nelson in Trafalgar Square.

Earlier Victoria had pressed a button and sent a personal message to her subjects. 'From my heart I thank my beloved people. May God bless them.' And by the modern wonder of the telegraph, her voice was carried to every corner of her glorious Empire.

As usual the papers forgot to mention the things that didn't quite go to plan. During the Diamond Jubilee the House of Commons wished to present a loyal address to the Queen. This involved the usual long-winded speeches by the Speaker of the House. But when the moment arrived the MPs disgraced themselves. In their eagerness to get a good look at Her Majesty, they nearly trampled her down in the rush. An eyewitness described the shocking scene:

> *The doors at the other end of the the ballroom were then opened and in came the House of Commons like a crowd being let on to the ground after a football match. . . This dishevelled mass of humanity came at the Queen, and instinctively the men of the Household felt that they were called upon to do or die. We moved out forming a protecting screen, and stemmed the tide while the Lord Chamberlain and Lord Steward tried to find the Speaker.*
>
> Frederick Ponsonby – Recollections of Three Reigns

You can imagine what Queen Victoria thought of this disgraceful behaviour and she didn't mince her words in telling her Ministers.

The Diamond Jubilee would be the last great party for the British Empire. Britain went into the First World

War as one of the richest countries in the world. By the end of the war the piggy bank would be empty and Britain would be in debt. In four years the country exhausted the riches of the Victorian age. It was a good job Victoria wouldn't be there to see her precious Empire go down the plug-hole.

The royal grandma

By 1899, the Queen was a grand old grandma of 80. She received between three and four thousand letters of congratulations on her birthday. She still joked about her age and said she felt quite young. Rheumatism in her legs meant she couldn't walk any more. A masseuse known as 'the Rubber' was employed to rub the royal legs. When Victoria wanted to get around she used her 'rolling chair' – a Victorian version of a wheelchair.

Sometimes a servant or member of the household was called to carry the fat little Queen from one room to another, chair and all. For short visits, Victoria would be pulled along in her donkey-drawn carriage. This wasn't such fun for her family who had to trot breathlessly along behind, trying to answer the Queen's questions.

It seemed as if she would go on for ever. At the age of 81 Victoria suddenly decided she'd make her first trip to

Ireland for 40 years. 'It is entirely my own idea,' she said, 'and I must confess it is not entirely to please the Irish, but partly because I expect to enjoy myself!' Despite the history of troubles between Britain and Ireland, Queen Victoria got a surprisingly warm welcome. In one village a woman yelled out, 'God bless the Queen!' 'And down with the Minister!' answered another voice from across the road.

The Queen's age began to show during the long, hot drives through the country and sometimes she dozed off on the journey. This posed a tricky problem, when a crowd of villagers was waiting to cheer the Queen. Fritz Ponsonby, her Assistant Private Secretary, got into the habit of digging his spurs into his horse to make it jump and whinny. The noise acted as an alarm call, either waking the dozy Queen or alerting Princess Beatrice to give her mother a dig in the royal ribs.

'HOW WE LAUGHED' – *Queen Victoria was amused*

Victoria's eyesight had been getting worse for some time. This led to some strange mix-ups. Once, when the Queen asked 'Where is Fritz [Ponsonby]?', Lord Balfour stepped forward, not having heard the question. The Queen, thinking she was talking to

Fritz, asked how his mother was. Balfour was rather stuck for an answer since his mother had been dead for some time.

Marie Mallet, a Lady in Waiting, also faced a delicate situation. In the evenings she would read the newspaper to the Queen who would often drop off to sleep. Marie was under strict instructions to keep Her Majesty awake. Should she grip the royal shoulders and give the Queen a good shake? Marie would try everything. . .

The new century dawned with the Queen in her 82nd year. The end was near. The old clock was at last running down. Death was in the air wherever Victoria looked. In July 1900 her second son, Alfie, died of cancer. Meanwhile in Germany, her eldest and favourite daughter was dying. Oddly enough Victoria, who had longed for death in the years after she lost Albert – now didn't want to call it a day.

After the Prince Consort's death I wished to die, but now I wish to live and do what I can for my country and those I love.

On Sunday January 13th 1901 Victoria made her last entry in her famous diary. It wasn't exactly dramatic stuff. . .

Had a fair night, but was a little wakeful. Got up earlier and had some milk. Out before one in the garden chair. . . Rested a little, had some food and took a short drive. . .

REAL DIARY EXTRACT

She had kept the diary for 70 years, from her 'sad dull childhood' through to her Diamond Jubilee and the new century. Now, in the last days of her life, it came to a sudden stop. Victoria went quickly downhill and the family gathered at her bedside.

On 21st January Bertie went to see his mother and speak to her. After he'd left the room, her doctor Sir James Reid stayed at her bedside. He was a bit surprised when the Queen kept kissing his hand.

Victoria evidently didn't realize that Bertie had gone and thought she was kissing her son's hand. Perhaps she was thinking about all the times she'd made his life a rotten misery.

The next day, Victoria faded fast – 'like a great three-decker ship sinking,' as one of her family said. Seeing Bertie she put out her arms and embraced him. She died in the arms of her grandson – Kaiser William of Germany – who not long after would start the First World War.

What were Victoria's famous last words? Some say they were, 'Oh Albert. . .' Maybe – after 40 years of mourning – she saw her dear hubby and was anxious to join him in heaven. The time had come for the final funeral. Victoria had some pretty odd ideas about that too.

There was one other item that few people knew about. A photo of her crusty old Scots servant – John Brown. It had to be placed in the Queen's left hand and cunningly hidden under some flowers. If Bertie had seen it he would have blown his top.

Victoria had dressed in black for 40 years but for her funeral she decided on a change.

THE HARD TIMES

1st February 1901

A WHITE FUNERAL FOR THE QUEEN

Queen Victoria was buried today in the white funeral she'd planned for herself.

The dead Queen wore her wedding veil for the occasion. It even snowed to make the day complete.

The Queen had requested a military funeral. However this backfired when the procession ran into a slight hitch. As the coffin was being pulled up the hill to Windsor Castle, the horses bucked and broke their harnesses. The rest of the procession went up the hill, unaware that they'd left Victoria's body behind!

It looked like a royal disaster until the navy stepped in to save the day. They got the King's permission to drag the gun carriage up the hill by rope.

'The damn navy ruined the ceremony,' grumbled the army commander, who was told to move his horses.

Victoria was buried side by side with her dear Albert at Frogmore. They're together again at last.

It was the end of an era. The close of the Victorian age. Victoria, for all her pig-headedness and stuffiness, had been a legend in her own lifetime. She was the Mother of the Empire, the Empress Queen who ruled over a quarter of the world's population. No mean achievement for a little old lady who rode about in a donkey carriage and wore a widow's cap instead of a crown.

Victorians queued up to write soppy verses about the Queen, while famous writers gave their own verdict:

I mourn the safe and motherly old middle-class Queen, who held the nation warm under the fold of her big hideous Scotch-plaid shawl.
The Great and the Good.
The Good and Human, the Likeable, the ever Lovable; and the Peculiar, the never Uninteresting.
HENRY JAMES, Novelist
Sir THEODORE MARTIN, Biographer of Albert
MAX BEERBOHM, Writer and cartoonist

In the end Victoria stood for everything both good and bad about the Victorian age. Strength, tradition, a stubborn will and an unswerving belief in Britain's greatness.

Bertie, or Edward VII (as he now became), would be different. Nicknamed Edward the Caresser, Bertie with his whiskers, hunting dog and strong whiff of cigar smoke, was ready to usher in a new era. The racey, fashionable, Edwardian age. And at long last – his interfering old mother wasn't there to stop him.